Welch D. Everman

WHO SAYS THIS?
The Authority of the Author, the Discourse, and the Reader

Southern Illinois University Press
CARBONDALE AND EDWARDSVILLE

Printed in the United States of America
Edited by Dan Gunter
Designed by Design for Publishing, Inc.
Production supervised by Linda Jorgensen-Buhman

91 90 89 88   4 3 2 1

Library of Congress Cataloging-in-Publication Data

Everman, Welch D., 1946–
    Who says this?: the authority of the author, the discourse, and
the reader/Welch D. Everman.
        p.   cm. — (Crosscurrents/modern critiques. Third series)
    Bibliography: p.
    Includes index.
    ISBN 0-8093-1444-4
    1. Literature. Modern — History and criticism. 2. Authority in
literature. I. Title. II. Series.
PN710.E9 1988
809'.03 — dc19   87-19285
                                                                  CIP

The paper used in this publication meets the minimum requirements
of American National Standard for Information Sciences -
Permanence of Paper for Printed Library Materials, ANSI
Z39.48-1984.

Contents

Crosscurrents/Modern Critiques/Third Series
Jerome Klinkowitz   vii

Acknowledgments   ix

Who Says This? An Introduction   xi

Part One
The Authority of the Author

1   The Novel as Document: The "Docufiction" of
Norman Mailer, Jay Cantor, and Jack Kerouac   3

2   The Man in Buffalo: Telling (,) the Teller (,)
and the Told in the Fiction of
Raymond Federman   34

Part Two
The Authority of the Discourse

3   Harry Mathews' *Selected Declarations of
Dependence*: Proverbs and the Forms
of Authority   65

4   The Word and the Flesh: The Infinite
Pornographic Text   78

v

Part Three
The Authority of the Reader

5   The Reader Who Reads and the Reader
        Who Is Read: A Reading of Italo Calvino's
        If on a winter's night a traveler   111
6   The Author and the I in the Fiction of
        J. L. Marcus   128
    Index   139

Crosscurrents/ Modern Critiques/ Third Series

IN THE EARLY 1960s, when the Crosscurrents/Modern series was developed by Harry T. Moore, the contemporary period was still a controversial one for scholarship. Even today the elusive sense of the present dares critics to rise above mere impressionism and to approach their subject with the same rigors of discipline expected in more traditional areas of study. As the first two series of Crosscurrents books demonstrated, critiquing contemporary culture often means that the writer must be historian, philosopher, sociologist, and bibliographer as well as literary critic, for in many cases these essential preliminary tasks are yet undone.

To the challenges that faced the initial Crosscurrents project have been added those unique to the past two decades: the disruption of conventional techniques by the great surge in innovative writing in the American 1960s just when social and political conditions were being radically transformed, the new worldwide interest in the Magic Realism of South American novelists, the startling experiments of textual and aural poetry from Europe, the emergence of Third World authors, the rising cause of feminism in life and literature, and, most dramatically, the introduction of Continental theory into the previously staid world of Anglo-American literary scholarship. These transformations demand that many traditional treatments be re-thought, and part of the new responsibility for Crosscurrents will be to provide such studies.

Contributions to Crosscurrents/Modern Critiques/Third Series will be distinguished by their fresh approaches to established topics and by their opening up of new territories for discourse. When a single author is studied, we hope to present the first book on his or her work or to explore a previously untreated aspect based on new research. Writers who have been critiqued well elsewhere will be studied in comparison with lesser-known figures, sometimes from other cultures, in an effort to broaden our base of understanding. Critical and theoretical works by leading novelists, poets, and dramatists will have a home in Crosscurrents/Modern Critiques/Third Series, as will sampler-introductions to the best in new Americanist criticism written abroad.

The excitement of contemporary studies is that all of its critical practitioners and most of their subjects are alive and working at the same time. One work influences another, bringing to the field a spirit of competition and cooperation that reaches an intensity rarely found in other disciplines. Above all, this third series of Crosscurrents/Modern Critiques will be collegial—a mutual interest in the present moment that can be shared by writer, subject, and reader alike.

Jerome Klinkowitz

Acknowledgments

My thanks go to John O'Brien of the *Review of Contemporary Fiction,* Robert Bonazzi of *Vortex,* and the editors of *Chicago Review* for permission to reprint essays that first appeared in those journals.

I also thank Bruce Jackson and Roy Roussel for inspiring a couple of these pieces; Robert Creeley for many good talks on the issue of literary authority; Dan Gunter, my editor at SIU Press; Jerome Klinkowitz, Larry McCaffery, Ray Federman, and my sister Nicole Bianco for being good sports (see the use and abuse of their good names in the "J. L. Marcus" essay); and Elizabeth Bard, my wife, for putting up with years of my living room lectures.

Who Says This?
An Introduction

THIS IS A COLLECTION OF essays written for a variety
of occasions or for no particular occasion at all. It is not a
coherent, book-length argument on the issue of literary
authority but an attempt to approach that issue from a
number of different perspectives. The collection provides no
single absolute answer because there is no single absolute
question.

For every statement, written or spoken, it makes sense to
ask: Who says this? The answer seems simple enough. The
speaker is the source of what he says. For the written text,
the one who says/writes this is the one whose name appears
on the title page, the author. Like the speaker, the author is
the source of his or her words.

In this sense, however, to be the source of language is not
to be the creator of language—the language with its
vocabulary, its rules of grammar and syntax, always preexists
every particular speaker or writer. Rather, it is to be a locus,
a place from which these particular words come, a specific

physical presence — the speaking apparatus, the writing hand. But this is not precisely what we want to know when we ask: Who says this? We want to know who — not which voice or hand but which person, which individual, which subject. And we want to know by what right, by what authority this person, this individual, this subject says what he says.

The question "Who says this?" raises many more questions. What do we mean by person, individual, subject as a source of words? In what sense can the individual speaker or writer be called individual when the words he speaks or writes are not his own but the common property of any number of speakers and writers, when in fact the very words he speaks or writes have been spoken and written any number of times before? Does the authority to say what he says come from without — as a judge receives the authorization to pass a sentence from a political order that is beyond him — or from within, from the individual mind or soul? In what sense, if any, can the spoken or the written be said to be accurate, useful, effective, true? Does the authority of the speaker or writer have its source in the truth of what is spoken or written, or is it authority itself that grounds the act of speaking or writing in truth? What is the source, the authorization, of authority?

These questions and innumerable others are posed here from the perspective of the one who receives what is spoken or written — the listener, the reader — but the speaker or writer can and perhaps should pose these questions as well. Traditionally, of course, these questions are not usually posed at all. In most cases, the authorization of authority seems to be clear, beyond question. The legislator, for example, is authorized to pronounce laws because her or she has been appointed or elected to that position (or has seized it) in and through the political system. The parent is authorized to discipline the child on the basis of legal and social conventions. The expert — the physician, the biologist, the psychologist, the critic — is authorized to pass judgment and to offer opinions on the basis of his or her education, experience, membership in authorizing groups, source of employment, etc.

The question of authority becomes much more difficult in the literary arena. What is the authority of the novelist, the poet? By what right does the novelist or the poet write? By what authority is one person recognized as a novelist while another is not? As posed by novelist, poet, and critic Harry Mathews, the question reads, quite simply, "What right have I to speak at all?"[1]

Again, traditionally, these questions are not usually posed. The source of literary authority already seems clear, beyond question. The author is an authority because of his or her ability to represent the world as it is in words. Or because the author is gifted with self expression, the ability to mine his or her own interiority and offer it in concrete form, as language. The author is the one who, unlike most of us, has something to say. Authority is grounded in artistry, in sensitivity, in genius. In a sense, the writer's authority is the authority of the parent — the author fathers his text.

The Author, when believed in, is always conceived of as the past of his own book: book and author stand automatically on a single line divided into a *before* and an *after*. The Author is thought to *nourish* the book, which is to say that he exists before it, thinks, suffers, lives for it, is in the same relation of antecedence to his work as a father to his child.[2]

1.   Harry Mathews, "Georges Perec," *Grand Street* 3 (Autumn 1983): 143.
2.   Roland Barthes, *Image/Music/Text,* trans. Stephen Heath (New York: Hill and Wang, 1977), 145.

This traditional definition of the author comes from Roland Barthes, from his crucial essay "The Death of the Author," in which he challenges the very possibility of literary authority. In truth, the traditional grounds of literary authority are certainly open to question, though traditionally the questions have not usually been asked.

Realists of the past and present (Emile Zola, Frank Norris, Norman Mailer) have believed and continue to believe in the ability of the author's words to represent the real, to reach the truth. In particular, the novel has been seen as such a vehicle to the real. But of course the novel is an established literary form, a form that preexists any given work. What then is the relationship, if any, between this form and the real that is to be represented? Is authority grounded in the form? If so, where does this leave the author who is therefore subordinate to the form which he or she does not create but merely realizes? But if authority is not rooted in the form of the novel, then what is its source?

Barthes argues that authority *is* rooted in literary forms, in the repetition of those forms, in the repetition of the already written. "The text is a tissue of quotations drawn from the innumerable centres of culture" (146). It is perhaps impossible to say whether or not there is some relationship between a particular discourse (say, the form of the novel) and a reality that is out there somewhere beyond language, but the authority of a given discourse clearly seems to be grounded in history, in a continual repetition of the past in the present. Most of the novels written today gain authority by repeating the recognizable form of traditional novelistic discourse, a form which is believed to be capable of mirroring the real.

But if history can bestow authority, it can also erode it. According to Jerome Klinkowitz, "much twentieth-century thought has worked for the overthrow of nineteenth-century

notions of realism."[3] Contemporary thinkers and artists have
lost faith in the idea of a correspondence between traditional
literary forms and the world, and the failure of realism has
led to the grounding of authority in the subjectivity of the
author. While writers of realistic fiction purposely attempted
to efface themselves in favor of a scientific objectivity, modern
writers find the very source of their work in themselves as subjects. Their art is self-expression.

The *author* still reigns in histories of literature, biographies of
writers, interviews, magazines, as in the very consciousness of men
of letters anxious to unite their person and their work through diaries
and memoirs. The image of literature to be found in ordinary
culture is tyrannically centered on the author, his person, his life,
his tastes, his passions, while criticism still consists for the most part
in saying that Baudelaire's work is the failure of Baudelaire the man,
Van Gogh's his madness, Tchaikovsky's his vice. The *explanation*
of a work is always sought in the man or woman who produced it,
as if it were always in the end, through the more or less transparent
allegory of the fiction, the voice of a single person, the *author* "con-
fiding" in us. (Barthes, 143)

But if the subjectivity of the author is to be the privileged
locus of authority, of self-expression, it is important to ask
about the nature of the subject. Maurice Blanchot has suggested that subjectivity "is merely a formal necessity: it simply
serves to allow the infinite relation of Self to Other."[4] But if
this is the case, if the Other is the source of subjectivity, then
the authority of the author who expresses "himself" or "herself"

3.   Jerome Klinkowitz, *The Self-Apparent Word: Fiction as Language/
     Language as Fiction* (Carbondale: Southern Illinois University Press,
     1984), 19.
4.   Maurice Blanchot, *The Writing of the Disaster*, trans. Ann Smock
     (Lincoln: University of Nebraska Press, 1986), 53.

comes not from within but from elsewhere, and what is expressed is not Self but the Other.

Art critic Hal Foster argues that "self-expression," like the realism that preceded it, is merely the realization of an established form, the playing out of a given discourse that has nothing to do with self or expression; "to express a self is largely to replicate a model."[5] For Barthes, to express the self is always to repeat the already expressed: "Did [the writer] wish to *express himself*, he ought at least to know that the inner thing he thinks to translate is itself only a ready-formed dictionary, its words only explainable through other words, and so on indefinitely" (146).

If realism and self-expression are both questionable possibilities in our postmodern era, if the author who has "something to say" can say only that which has already been said, with no guarantee that what is said has any relationship to anything we might want to call the real or the self, then what is the source of authority? How does one begin to answer the question: Who says this? It is becoming painfully obvious that this introduction is not providing a resolution to the various problems of literary authority, and—for better or worse—the same is true of the essays to follow, which certainly raise many more quesitons than they answer.

The first two essays address the issue of documentation in the novel, one through a look at "docufiction"—what Norman Mailer has called "the true life novel"—and the other through an analysis of the "failed" autobiographical novels of Raymond Federman. In part 2, "The Authority of Discourse," I look at the question of authority with regard to two established discursive realms which seem to be, in a very real sense, authorless—pornography and proverbs.

5. Hal Foster, "The Expressive Fallacy," *Art in America* 71 (January 1983): 82.

Italo Calvino's fictions also draw on established discursive genres which always seem to subordinate the author to the form — science fiction, the boys' adventure tale, the detective story, etc. — but his novel *If on a winter's night a traveler* is one of the few works of fiction that implicates the reader directly in the question of authority. For Barthes, "the true place of the writing . . . is reading" (p.147), and the essay on Calvino explores this possibility.

The last piece in the collection also explores the authority of the reader/critic, but this "essay" is admittedly a fiction — there is no novelist named J. L. Marcus, no Marcus text, and many (but not all) of the works cited do not exist. How these facts or the lack of them might influence the argument, I cannot say. I cannot even say who is saying/writing this piece on J. L. Marcus, though the voice of the narrator/critic is familiar. The problem here is the problem faced by anyone who addresses the issue of authority and who does so in writing. Who says this? By what authority? "What right have I to speak at all?"

Part One

The Authority of the Author

1

The Novel as Document:
The "Docufiction" of Norman Mailer,
Jay Cantor, and Jack Kerouac

WHAT DOES IT MEAN TO SAY that a novel — a work of fiction — is based on the life of a real person, on events that really happened in the world beyond the page? On the one hand, it seems safe to say that most if not all works of fiction are based, more or less, on real persons and real events, or on persons and events that might be real, transformed through the imagination of the author. On the other hand, however, when an author wants to write about "the real world" and to convince his readers that his text somehow corresponds to factual events, he usually uses one of the various forms of nonfiction — biography, history, journalism, etc. But there are also many texts that call themselves novels and that are read as novels but that purport to be about the real — e.g., the autobiographical novels of Henry Miller and Louis-Ferdinand

Céline, Hermann Broch's *The Death of Virgil*, Robert Coover's *The Public Burning* (based on the espionage trial and execution of the Rosenbergs), and countless historical novels and fictional biographies like Howard Fast's *Spartacus* and *Citizen Tom Paine*. But in what sense, if any, can such works, which for the most part accept the rules of novelistic discourse, be said to say something about the real persons and events on which they are based?

Norman Mailer's *The Executioner's Song* is, according to the subtitle, "A True Life Novel." But which is the key term? True? Life? Novel? There would seem to be a built-in contradiction here. It isn't unusual to say that a novel—by definition, a work of fiction—is *like* life, that it reads as if it *could* be true, that it is very realistic. But Mailer seems to be making a very different claim. He writes: "This book does its best to be a factual account of the activities of Gary Gilmore and the men and women associated with him in the period from April 9, 1976, when he was released from the United States Penitentiary at Marion, Illinois, until his execution a little more than nine months later in Utah State Prison."[1]

Mailer calls the book both a novel and "a factual account," and the text is full of real dates and the names of real people and real places. But which is it, fact or fiction? Of course, *The Executioner's Song* is not the first attempt on the part of a novelist to tell a "true life" story in the form of fiction. Almost any traditional historical novel does the same thing by placing its fictive characters and situations within a context of real names, places, dates, and events. But it would seem that Mailer wants to claim that *The Executioner's Song* is not simply a historical novel, based on very recent history. It is,

1. Norman Mailer, *The Executioner's Song* (New York: Warner, 1980), 1020. Hereafter cited as *Song*.

rather, a "story . . . as accurate as one can make it" (*Song*, 1020). It is, paradoxically, a factual fiction.

The story Mailer choses for his "true life novel" was already well known to most Americans before he began work on the book. It was, as they say, in all the papers. Gary Gilmore, recently released from prison where he had spent most of his life, committed two senseless murders in Provo, Utah, was convicted, and was sentenced to death. Gilmore's story became a media event when he refused to appeal the sentence and asked to be executed. Regardless of Gilmore's personal motives, his request was, in effect, an act of rebellion against the legal system which is designed to allow condemned criminals to continue to live on almost inexhaustible appeals. In a sense, Gilmore was insisting that the state, having condemned him to death, follow through on its demand — indeed, that it assist him in taking his own life via legal channels. Gilmore's acceptance of his execution was also an act of rebellion against opponents of the death penalty and against a Supreme Court decision that had put capital punishment into question without resolving the issue in any clear sense. The fact is that, at the time of Gilmore's execution in 1977, no one had been put to death in the United States for more than a decade, though capital punishment laws were still on the books in most states and many convicts were still awaiting execution.

In other words, Gilmore's story was already a story before Mailer started work on *The Executioner's Song* — a story that had been told again and again in police reports, in legal documents, in court transcripts, and in the press. It was, indeed, a story that Mailer already knew from his own writing, a story that, in a sense, he had already written. In the late 1950s, in an essay entitled "The White Negro," Mailer wrote: "[I]f the fate of twentieth-century man is to live with death from adolescence to premature senescence, why then the only life-giving answer is to accept the terms of death, to live with death as immediate danger, to divorce oneself from society, to exist without roots, to set out on that uncharted journey with the rebellious imperatives of the self."[2]

This is Gilmore's story, written by Mailer two decades before Gilmore's death, which merely brought to closure the original text. For our purposes here, it doesn't matter what the real Gary Gilmore thought he was doing or why he acted as he did. It is unlikely that anyone will ever know that—certainly Norman Mailer does not know, and *The Executioner's Song* does not make Gary Gilmore's motives or thoughts particularly coherent. Gilmore remains a mystery.

What is interesting here, however, is that Mailer, in *The Executioner's Song*, is rewriting a story that he himself has already written and that he is using that original story (which preexists Gary Gilmore's story) to tell again a story that has already been told repeatedly by any number of tellers. And this story—admittedly cast in the traditional form of fiction and told at second-, third-, fourth-, nth-hand—is what Mailer calls "a factual account," a "true life novel."

The Executioner's Song raises some important questions. First, why has Mailer decided to try to reach the reality of Gary Gilmore through the form of the novel rather than through the more conventional forms of journalism, biography, etc.? Why has he chosen to involve himself in the paradoxical effort of writing a *"true life story,* with its real names and real lives—as if it were a novel" (*Song*, 1022)?

What Mailer is doing here represents what could be called a discursive shift—a conscious shift from journalistic or biographical discourse, the kind of discourse that his material suggests, to a novelistic discourse. Tzvetan Todorov has noted

2. Norman Mailer, *Advertisements for Myself* (New York: Berkley Medallion, 1966), 312-13.

that "[a] particular type of discourse is . . . defined by the list of rules which it must obey,"[3] and in *The Executioner's Song* Mailer chooses to follow the rules of fiction rather than those of nonfiction — a strange choice, given that his goal is not fiction but reality, the truth.

There seems to be a sense in which Mailer believes that the novel is somehow "truer" to life than the various discourses of nonfiction. And it is certainly the case that novelistic discourse allows the writer far more flexibility than, say, journalistic or biographical discourse. Novelistic discourse is, quite simply, more complete than the discourses of nonfiction. According to Felix Martinez-Bonati, "Novelistic discourse will catch our attention and distinguish itself, if at all, not by deficiency but by perfection, by the apparent thoroughness of the presentation of the objects in reference."[4]

This "perfection," this "thoroughness," seems to be what Mailer is after. It is the key to the "truer truth" of the novel over the journalistic account or the biography. It is worth noting here that Mailer never seems to lose confidence in the authority of novelistic discourse or in his own authority as a writer to get to the really real, to the "true life story" of Gary Gilmore. The question is, however: Is his confidence justified? Can novelistic discourse ever reach something we might want to call the real, a reality that presumably exists beyond discourse, beyond words?

The Executioner's Song exploits the full range of possibilities that novelistic discourse allows but that the discourses of nonfiction do not, and chief among them is the possibility of authorial omniscience. Mailer does not appear in the text as

3. Tzvetan Todorov, "The Notion of Literature," *New Literary History* 5 (Autumn 1973): 14.
4. Felix Martinez-Bonati, "The Act of Writing Fiction," *New Literary History* 11 (Spring 1980): 425.

a participant in the action or as the author, and the text never reflects on itself, apart from the brief afterword that is, in fact, set outside *The Executioner's Song* proper. The teller of the story is an omniscient narrator, capable of entering the minds of his characters.

In one scene, chosen almost at random from the text, Gilmore's cousin Brenda is testifying against him in court. Mailer writes: "Oh, Gary, said Brenda in her heart, Don't be so angry with me. My testimony means nothing" (*Song*, 432 − 33). The text here is clearly within the realm of novelistic discourse but well outside the discourses of nonfiction, where it would be impossible, within the established rules, to recount what a real person said to herself "in her heart." It is Mailer's choice of a novelistic discourse that allows him to make such a narrative move.

Novelistic discourse also allows Mailer to record dialogues between characters not as transcriptions − for many of the dialogues in *The Executioner's Song* no transcriptions exist, because they were never recorded − but as if they were taking place before the reader's eyes/ears. Here, Brenda visits Gary in prison after he has made an unsuccessful attempt at suicide by drug overdose.

Back at the window, Brenda couldn't stop herself. The guard might just as well have egged her on. "Hey, Gary," she said, "how come you didn't take enough to do the job?"

"What makes you think I didn't?" said Gary.

"If you had," said Brenda, "you'd have been dead."

"What in the hell are you trying to do? You know I really meant to do it."

Brenda said, "You know more about drugs than that. I think you knew just what you were doing."

Gary started to tuck his lip in. Finally, he kind of snickered, and said, "Well, I might know one of my cousins would pick up on that."

Yet, in the way he said it, she was confused. He was perfectly capable of letting her think she was right when she was wrong. Gary liked to toy with her head. (*Song*, 608)

This is a fascinating passage, not as novelistic discourse per se but as a novelistic discourse that hopes to reach the reality of what happened in this particular confrontation. Let's assume for the moment that every word of the dialogue is recounted here as it actually happened — that every word between the quotation marks was actually said. Thus far, the dialogue could be an element of novelistic or nonfiction discourse. But phrases like "Brenda couldn't stop herself," "Gary started to tuck his lip in," and "she was confused" put the discourse beyond the realm of nonfiction, because they recount what only an omniscient onlooker could record. Again, this is an advantage of novelistic over nonfiction discourse, one of the key elements that makes traditional realistic fiction realistic.

In *The Executioner's Song*, Mailer also develops a narrative voice that, while omniscient, manages to slide in and out of various characters' thoughts effortlessly by momentarily adopting a character's personal tone. The narrative voice allows the reader to move into the mind of a character so easily that it seems perfectly natural. "Julie had to stay in the hospital one more night, so Craig Taylor was still alone. He was just putting the kids to sleep, when Gary knocked on the door and introduced his girl as Nicole's sister, April. They looked odd. Not drunk, but the girl was in bad shape. Paranoid. She couldn't sit down. Walked around Craig like he was a barrel or something."

The passage shows a clear discursive shift from nonfiction to the novel. "Julie had to stay in the hospital one more night, so Craig Taylor was still alone" can be read as a statement of simple fact, as nonfiction. But in the very next sentence, Mailer sets up the discursive shift in the phrase "this girl." A narrrator recounting the scene from the outside would probably say "a girl." "This girl" subtly shifts the narrative into Craig's mind, and from "They looked odd" on, everything said represents Craig's judgments in his own imprecise, nonauthorial voice ("like a barrel *or something*"), despite the fact that these judgments are recounted not in Craig's voice directly but in the third person.

Passages like this one seem to be located in the gray area between novelistic and nonfiction discourse, though in fact they are purely novelistic insofar as they clearly transcend the rules of nonfiction. Mailer's subtle (and indeed only apparent) discursive shifts within the text do make the story highly realistic. But can such a strategy make the move from the real*istic* to the real?

Mailer's choice of novelistic discourse for the telling of Gilmore's story allows for a completeness and a kind of immediacy that is not available in the discourses of nonfiction. But "the illusion of immediacy that is so essential to *realistic* fiction is just what makes the narrative incredible as soon as we attempt to read it as a report of real facts (Martinez-Bonati, 426).

There is a contradiction at the heart of a novelistic discourse that hopes to be not merely realistic but "a report of real facts." As such an intended report, Mailer's text recounts the impossible — primarily, the inner workings of other minds. Impossibilities of this sort are, of course, precisely the possibilities of novelistic discourse. Again, according to Martinez-Bonati, "In presenting events, novelistic discourse tends to assume a point of view whose possibility is excluded precisely by their very nature" (425). But, certainly, the possibility of impossibility is exactly what makes a novelistic discourse not reality but fiction.

The Executioner's Song, then, seems doomed to failure, not as a novel but as a "true life story." Mailer understands this risk. At least he seems to understand that the realism of novelistic discourse per se is not going to get the job done as he wants it done. And so, while he does not seem to question the authority of novelistic discourse, he introduces techniques within that discourse that are designed to force the novelistic text to transcend itself in the direction of the real.

This is precisely why there are so many documents included in *The Executioner's Song*, documents that Mailer himself did not write. His text incorporates many other textual elements of Gary Gilmore's story—legal transcripts and transcripts of taped interviews, letters written by Gilmore to his girlfriend Nicole and her replies, Nicole's will, and newspaper accounts of the Gilmore case which are scattered throughout the text, with a number of them gathered together in a chapter suitably entitled "Testaments."

The point here is to force a text already committed to novelistic discourse—Mailer's portion of *The Executioner's Song*—to transcend itself, to go beyond its own discourse and into the discourse of the "real" via documents from the world outside the text. And indeed, these documents—the letters, the transcripts, the newspaper reports—are not elements of novelistic discourse. They come to the novel from the real world.

The documents in *The Executioner's Song* are quotations from sources outside the novelistic text—that they come from without is the whole point. But, for Mailer as for any writer, to quote is always to quote out of context, to lift a text out of its original context and place it somewhere else. As such, the documents included in *The Executioner's Song*, while not written by Mailer, become part of Mailer's novelistic discourse. They do not open the novel into the real word; they draw documents of the real world into the discourse of the novel.

But if the inclusion of documents fails to put the text beyond its own novelistic discourse, Mailer has another strategy which violates one of the fundamental rules of the discourse he has chosen for Gilmore's story. Novelistic discourse is perfect, at least when compared to the discourses of nonfiction. And the possibility of its perfection is based on selectivity. In fact, every discourse is selective — it says what it says rather than the potentially infinite number of things it might have said but does not.

In *The Executioner's Song*, Mailer tries to transcend his own novelistic discourse by refusing to be selective, by trying to say everything. There are no minor details in the text. Everything is important or seems to be. For example, Mailer's descriptions are far more detailed than any theory of novelistic discourse might demand. "Big Jake came back to the tank with a large jar of instant coffee, a large jar of Tang, and a carton of Gibbs' brand of cigarettes, Viceroy Super Longs" (*Song*, 644).

Mailer gives his characters the same exhaustive treatment. There are no minor characters here. Each is provided with a background, a personal history, even a psychological profile. In his introduction of Utah County prosecutor Noall Wooten, Mailer writes: "In Noall Wooten's opinion the best lawyer he ever met was his father. Maybe for that reason he could never go into a courtroom without a stomach tied in knots" (*Song*, 276). This characterization — which is far more complete than the fragment quoted above — is totally superfluous. Wooten's actual part in the novel is not large enough to warrant it. And yet, again and again, Mailer attempts to exhaust even the most minor characters, to say everything about them. He seems to agree with producer Larry Schiller, another "real" character in the novel, who says: "Take down everything and anything, even your legal discussions. Talk about the will. It's all part of history. You never know when it's going to be important" (*Song*, 699-700).

Mailer does include everything and anything, because he never knows when it is going to be important. That is, he cannot know which detail might be precisely the one that will transform his novel into something no longer fictional but true. In fact, by trying to avoid selecting, by trying to say everything, Mailer seems to be trying to transcend not merely novelistic discourse but discourse itself. He seems to believe that if he can indeed say absolutely everything, if he can exhaust discourse completely, then he can reach a reality that is out there somewhere on the far side of language. It is as if, in this process of piling up words, details, phrases, sentences, quotations, the text might eventually collapse under its own weight like a dead star, leaving only a black hole behind. And this black hole would be the truth, the real.

But of course, Mailer cannot hope to succeed, because he cannot hope to say everything, to write until the possibilities of language are exhausted. The text that would say absolutely everything would be an infinite text, a text not only without end but without beginning, a text that would have always already begun, that would always be in medias res. Such a text would be a complete impossibility, and even a novelistic discourse—which makes the impossible possible—cannot transcend itself by exhausting itself.

Norman Mailer intends his work to be read as truth, as a discourse on reality, as the real itself. But, according to Martinez-Bonati, the author's intentions have nothing to do with how a text is read.

Novelistic texts force us, by the nature of the sentences they contain, to read in the corresponding key. Therefore, it is not a matter of the intention of the author whether a text is to be read as a novel or not . . . if [a text] lends itself to be read successfully as a novel, and not as a historiographical narrative or as an autobiography, it is the text of a novel—regardless of the theoretical possibility that the author, victim of a strange disturbance, might have wanted something else. (Martinez-Bonati, 433 – 34)

Despite his conscious choice of a novelistic discourse, with all its advantages over the discourses of nonfiction, Norman Mailer certainly did want and expect something else of *The Executioner's Song*. He wanted the book to be read as "a factual account," the truth. And yet, despite his intention to write a "true life story," *The Executioner's Song* remains, hopelessly, a novel, a fiction.

Failure seems to be built into the very idea of a "true life novel," and though Mailer seems to see the risks involved — this is precisely why he develops various strategies for getting beyond his own novelistic discourse — he does not seem to recognize that failure is inevitable.

In his novel, *The Death of Che Guevara*, Jay Cantor faces many of the same problems Mailer had to deal with — or failed to deal with — in *The Executioner's Song*. Cantor's novel presents the life of the Latin American Revolutionary from his childhood in Argentina to his death in Bolivia, and the intent — like Mailer's — would seem to be to capture the truth of Ernesto Guevara in words.

By the time Mailer began to write about him, Gary Gilmore was already a media figure. It often happens with names in the news, however, that they disappear from the public mind as quickly as they came on the scene, and today it is not likely that many Americans remember Gary Gilmore or why he made headlines — unless, of course, they are readers of Norman Mailer. Che Guevara, on the other hand, was and remains an almost legendary figure in many parts of the world. He was second-in-command to Fidel Castro during the Cuban revolution, became the chronicler of that revolution and a foremost expert on guerilla warfare, held high offices in the new Cuban government, left Cuba to pursue revolutionary activities in the Congo, in Algeria, and elsewhere around the world, and died in the attempt to initiate a continent-wide revolution in Bolivia. Gary Gilmore, in the last analysis, was a small-time criminal and no doubt best forgotten. Che Guevara, on the other hand, was, in the words of Fidel Castro, "a seed which will give rise to many men determined to imitate him, men determined to follow his example."[5]

Still, Gilmore and Guevara have something in common. Both seem to fit the description of the hipster/outsider from Mailer's "White Negro" essay. In fact, far more than Gilmore, Guevara knew how "to accept the terms of death, to live with death as immediate danger, to divorce oneself from society, to exist without roots, to set out on that uncharted journey with the rebellious imperatives of the self." Indeed, it is precisely Guevara's sense of being-toward-death that makes him interesting.

Gilmore's life, at least near the end, became the subject of much documentation — legal, journalistic, and otherwise. He even attempted to document himself in letters, interviews, poems. The same is true for Guevara, who has been the subject of biographies, historical works, legal and governmental documents, and intelligence reports, and who also wrote a number of important books himself — *Guerilla Warfare, Reminiscences of the Cuban Revolutionary War, Venceremos!,* a collection of speeches and writings, and the posthumously published *Complete Bolivian Diaries of Che Guevara and Other Captured Documents.* Again, far more than Gilmore, Guevara, at the time of his death in 1967, already existed as a story told by many tellers, including himself.

Given the status of his subject, it might seem that Jay Cantor would choose the mode of biographical discourse for his work. But he does not. *The Death of Che Guevara* is a novel, not

5. Fidel Castro, "El Che Vive!" *Evergreen* 12 (February 1968): 35.

only because it says so on the title page but because Cantor takes the kind of liberties that are only possible in novelistic discourse. As we've seen, this choice provides some interesting advantages in the telling of the tale, but it also sets the narrative beyond what we might want to call the reality of Che Guevara. Again, as with *The Executioner's Song*, the reader of *The Death of Che Guevara* must ask: In what sense can a novel about Che Guevara reach the truth?

Before turning to *The Death of Che Guevara*, it might be interesting to look at a treatment of Guevara's life and work set within the traditional limits of biographical discourse. Andrew Sinclair's *Che Guevara* is a good example. Here, the discourse never enters the mind and thoughts of Che Guevara, as a novel might and as, indeed, Cantor's novel does. Sinclair reports facts. "Born into a privileged family of Spanish and Irish descent in 1928, Ernesto Guevara de la Serna was to react strongly enough from his background."[6]

Sinclair also reports what others have said of Guevara in documents, along with what Guevara had to say about himself in his own writings. Sinclair is not above interpreting the information that exists about his subject — that, in fact, is his job as a critical biographer. Thus, he feels that he can "sum up" Guevara, based on the information at hand.

This was the background of a revolutionary. First, a family that felt itself cut off from other privileged families by its consciousness of social inequalities. Then a personal temperament that was intelligent, mature, rebellious, and stubborn. Then a wandering over a continent where successions of bad governments had made mass poverty stink in the nostrils and shame the eyes. Then a doctor's concern for curing the incurable millions, whose diseases were only their symptoms, since the root cause was social injustice. Then a

6.   Andrew Sinclair, *Che Guevara* (New York: Viking, 1970), 1.

personal experience of three failed revolutions — the Bolivian revolution, later to be overthrown by an army *Putsch*; the Guatemalan revolution, destroyed by an imperialist intervention; and the Mexican revolution, rotted by internal sloth and decay. This experience changed a young doctor, whose nature was radical, into a revolutionary by intent. He had moved from passive indignation to active resistance, from observing to planning. His sympathy for suffering humanity had become a strategy for finding the remedy for that suffering. (Sinclair, 13 — 14)

The above is squarely within the framework of biographical discourse. Sinclair always writes of Guevara from the outside, from the standpoint of an observer and researcher, basing his interpretations and conclusions on documentary evidence. For our purposes, whether those interpretations and conclusions are correct or not is beside the point. What is important is that Sinclair limits himself to the documents that already exist. And what he has written is, in fact, yet another document on the life of Che Guevara.

On the other hand, *The Death of Che Guevara* is not such a document, although Cantor's novel, like Sinclair's biography, depends upon the existence of other documents and draws information and even direct quotations from them again and again. What makes Cantor's novel different from Sinclair's book — and from Mailer's — is its response to the question of authority.

Mailer never seems to question the authority of novelistic discourse to tell the truth about Gary Gilmore. Likewise, Andrew Sinclair never questions the authority of biographical discourse to present the truth about Che Guevara. Cantor, like Mailer, has chosen the novel as his form, and, on the surface at least, he seems to assume even a greater authority than Mailer, who tells his story from the perspective of an omniscient narrator. Most of Cantor's novel is told in the first person, in Guevara's own voice. In fact, the bulk of the text poses as Guevara's own writings, though of course these writings — for the most part — were written not by the historical Che Guevara but by novelist Jay Cantor. It would seem, then, that Cantor assumes the authority to speak not only *for* Che Guevara but *as* Che Guevara.

But who is speaking here? Not the historical Che Guevara, certainly, because he is dead. And not Jay Cantor. As Michel Foucault has explained:

It is well known that in a novel narrated in the first person, neither the first person pronoun, the present indicative tense, nor, for that matter, its signs of localization refer directly to the writer, either to the time when he wrote, or to the specific act of writing; rather they stand for a "second self" whose similarity to the author is never fixed and undergoes considerable alteration within the course of a single book. It would be as false to seek the author in relation to the actual writer as to the fictional narrator; the "author-function" arises out of their scission — in the division and distance of the two.[7]

Here, Foucault puts the authority of the author into question, and it is a question that the text of *The Death of Che Guevara* must address. Indeed, Cantor's text *does* question the authority of its author: "In the intervals of silence I lost myself, felt myself falling into the silence, like an unraveling, the letters that made up my name scattering all over the page. I didn't know who he was he means I am."[8] According to Foucault, the first person narrator/author here is not Jay Cantor, nor is it Che Guevara. It is a fictional narrator, a fictional author, a fictional Che Guevara. But the confusion of pro-

7. Michel Foucault, *Language, Counter-Memory, Practice,* trans. Donald F. Bouchard and Sherry Simon (Ithaca: Cornell University Press, 1980), 129.
8. Jay Cantor, *The Death of Che Guevara* (New York: Vintage, 1984), 117. Hereafter cited as *Guevara.*

nouns suggests that the author(s), the narrator(s), and the historical character have collapsed into each other. "I didn't know who he was he means I am." In this strange sentence, the "I" gives authority to the "he," only to take it back again by explaining what "he" means. But is this Cantor writing about the fictional Che, the fictional Che writing about his "real" author, Jay Cantor, or a strange collaboration between author and character? And what of the "real" Che Guevara?

In fact, the passage suggests that the author (Guevara? Cantor?) exists only on paper — "the letters that made up my name scattering all over the page." Foucault has suggested as much concerning writing in general.

[T]he writing of our day has freed itself from the necessity of "expression"; it only refers to itself, yet it is not restricted to the confines of interiority. On the contrary, we recognize it in its exterior deployment. This reversal transforms writing into an interplay of signs, regulated less by the content it signifies than by the very nature of the signifier. Moreover, it implies an action that is always testing the limits of its regularity, transgressing and reversing an order that it accepts and manipulates. (Writing unfolds like a game that inevitably moves beyond its own rules and finally leaves them behind. Thus, the essential basis of this writing is not the exalted emotions related to the act of composition or the insertion of a subject into language. Rather, it is primarily concerned with creating an opening where the writing subject endlessly disappears.) (Foucault, 116)

The above can be applied directly to the text of *The Death of Che Guevara*. Like Mailer, Cantor disappears behind the text, but within the text the writing subject is a fictional Che Guevara, a Guevara who exists only on the page, as a signifier. This Guevara's writings, however, are an amalgamation of writings by the historical Che Guevara (his Bolivian diaries) and the writings of the fictional Che Guevara (which Cantor has written for him). Like Mailer, Cantor incorporates other documents, documents he did not write, into the text of the novel, though he does not distinguish between these "outside" writings and his own. That is to say, he does not let the reader know when he is quoting and when he is inventing. This collaboration between Cantor and Guevara, or rather between the fictional Guevara and the factual Guevara, is a fascinating example of what Foucault means when he says that writing is always "transgressing and reversing an order that it accepts and manipulates." This collaboration is a way for Cantor to remain within his chosen novelistic discourse and to move beyond it at the same time, perhaps in an effort to get at the reality of Che Guevara.

But where is the reality here? As a fictive nonfictional novel, the text of *The Death of Che Guevara* is even more complicated than this collaboration suggests. There is another narrator here, sometimes called Walter, sometimes Ponco. He too is a first-person narrator, a writer writing about Che, collecting Che's writings (real and imaginary), and commenting on those writings after Guevara's death "From now on," Ponco writes, "*my* life will be to tell *his* story" (*Guevara*, 311). But in the process, this survivor of the abortive Bolivian campaign also manages to write about himself as well.

The novel, then, is multilayered, with the levels continually bleeding into one another. Cantor writes a text composed by the fictive Guevara and rewrites a text already written by the historical Guevara. Ponco, a character within the novel, rewrites these texts in turn and writes his own commentary texts at the same time. There is even the indication that Ponco (like Cantor) would like to alter the texts of Guevara to suit himself.

Can I change things—depending on how *he* felt to me, how I felt about him?

What about *history*?
Can I change his words? I know how to mimic his style. (*Guevara*,
362)

Of course, the moment the reader realizes that Ponco can
mimic Guevara's style and that he is considering changing
what Guevara wrote, the entire text becomes open to question. Who is writing this? Cantor? Guevara (real or imagined)?
Ponco? And, indeed, what about *history*? With its many layers
of authors, each altering the texts of the others, the strange
assemblage of documents and pseudodocuments that is *The
Death of Che Guevara* seems to move farther and farther from
the reality of its subject and deeper and deeper into the realm
of fiction.

The character Guevara also contributes to the questioning
of the text. Some of his writings are attempts to analyze, to
criticize, to document himself. But, inevitably, these self-
documents are failures.

Self-criticism: crossing parts of myself out, rewriting myself. Instead of killing myself or my comrades, a metaphorical way to
sacrifice myself.
"Sacrifice myself" — more rhetoric! Cross it out. (*Guevara*, 23)

In the above passage, Guevara seems to understand that he
is only a textual being, that he can be rewritten — by himself
and perhaps by others. Here, he criticizes not only himself
but his manner of writing himself into existence. And, in the
text of novel, the above passage is crossed over, canceled,
though it is still legible. This passage of self-criticism, excluded
from the text and yet included at the same time, again calls
the entire work into question. What, if anything, is true here?

Again and again, the text of *The Death of Che Guevara*
reflects on itself *as text*, as an "ambiguous story told by some

North American" (*Guevara*, 562). The implication here is that this is only a story, only a text that cannot reach beyond itself to get at the truth of Che Guevara, a text that, in Foucault's words, "only refers to itself." Cantor acknowledges this openly by structuring the text in such a way that it is impossible to know what has been written by whom, thus making it absolutely impossible to move with assurance from the textual realm to the realm of fact.

And yet the closed nature of the text, the avowed storiness of the story, is precisely the point. The life of Che Guevara is a story, nothing more and nothing less, which has been and can be written and rewritten by innumerable authors. The story existed before Cantor came to (re)write his own version, and it continues to exist in countless versions in the minds of all the people who know of Guevara's life. In a sense, there is no Che Guevara beyond the stories Cantor, Ponco, Fidel Castro, Andrew Sinclair, and the rest of us tell. *The Death of Che Guevara*, then, cannot reach the real Che Guevara, because that real Guevara does not exist, and perhaps never did. And so, the fictive Guevara in Cantor's novel can write: "For I liked being *an interesting character*. It promised a rich fate; a good story" (*Guevara*, 148). And Ponco can voice his own suspicions about the ill-fated Bolivian campaign: "And I think that our death in those mountains was part of the story, an ending that Che wanted written" (*Guevara*, 545).

The truth about Guevara is, quite simply, not available, though it is possible to speculate on what that truth might be. In Ponco's words: "There must be an account that isn't distorted by the use someone is making of him, a report called *the truth*. What God saw. Or is God just another point of view—the propaganda of heaven? the holy ideology?" (*Guevara*, 551).

"What God saw" might be the truth, but there is no way of getting at it. As Mailer failed to reach the reality of Gary

Gilmore, Cantor fails to reach the reality of Che Guevara. The difference is that Cantor knows he is failing, that he must fail, that failure is built into the project, and he admits it. In this sense, then, Cantor's false document is somehow truer than Mailer's because, while both writers invent, imagine, even lie, Cantor acknowledges that he is lying, and a liar who, in the process of lying, admits that he is lying is at some level telling the truth. But in the text of the novel the fictive Guevara opens even this minimal truth to question. "I had written me, and if I'd lied, were my lies, as I'd hoped, like some psychoanalytic sympton, an indirect way back to what was central? Had I, as I thought I wished, betrayed myself? Or was it just another story, one of so many possible, with me (whoever that was) excluded, outside, just another reader of an arbitrary epic?" (*Guevara*, 153).

The Death of Che Guevara call the entire enterprise of "docufiction" into question, and it does so by accepting novelistic discourse as its form, then deconstructing that form from within. Jack Kerouac, on the other hand, uses deconstructive techniques within novelistic discourse not to question the possibility of capturing the real in words but, hopefully, to make it happen, to transcend the text at last in favor of the real.

Jack Kerouac writes in the space between fiction and nonfiction, and all of his works are to be read there. His huge book *Visions of Cody* — like *The Executioner's Song* and *The Death of Che Guevara* — is an attempt to document the reality of a single person, Neal Cassady, who appears in the book under the name Cody Pomeray. But unlike Gary Gilmore and Che Guevara, Cassady was not a celebrity — at least, he wasn't one when Kerouac wrote *Visions of Cody* in 1952, though, precisely because of Kerouac's books, he became something of a hero to the Beats of the fifties and the hippies of the sixties. This is an important difference because, while Mailer and

Cantor try to capture the truth of characters who have already created themselves and whose lives are finished, Kerouac is attempting to capture the truth of a life that is still in the process of being lived. And, because Cassady is not a public figure, Kerouac must proceed without the kind of documentation that already existed for Gilmore and Guevara before Mailer and Cantor began their own experiments in documentation. There is a sense in which Kerouac must create Cassady/Pomeray as he goes along.

Also while Mailer and Cantor never met Gilmore or Guevara and in fact came to know their characters through their own acts of documentation, Kerouac is trying to document someone he knows well, his best friend, indeed someone he deifies and fears.

Cody was so great, so good, that I couldn't believe it—he was by far the greatest man I had ever known. . . . But enough of my greatest enemy—because while I saw him as an angel, a god, etcetera, I also saw him as a devil, an old witch, even an old bitch from the start and always did think and still do that he can read my thoughts and interrupts them on purpose *so I'll look on the world like he does.*[9] [Italics in original]

Kerouac, then, has a vital and personal stake in the documentation of Cassady, because it is, at the same time, the documentation of himself, an essential element in "this lifelong monologue which is begun in my mind" (*Cody*, 99) that calls for "an endless contemplation" (98). Kerouac, then, is a character *in* this text as well as a product *of* it—he is both the teller and the told. If it is true that Kerouac is somehow forced to look on the world as Cassady does, then, by ex-

---

9.   Jack Kerouac, *Visions of Cody* (New York: McGraw-Hill, 1972), 298.
     Hereafter cited as *Cody*.

hausting Cassady in his document, Kerouac may also succeed in documenting and understanding himself. Despite the differences, Gilmore, Guevara, and Cassady have much in common. All three are outsiders, each in his own way. All three defy law and the social order. All three seem to live by their own definitions of dignity and morality — at least as they are documented in the texts by Mailer, Cantor, and Kerouac. Mailer's definition of the hipster, which applies so well to both Gilmore and Guevara, also applies to Cassady, and, in fact, Mailer could very well have had Neal Cassady in mind when he wrote "The White Negro" and his other hipster essays. In the late forties and early fifties Cassady was the ultimate hipster, the living embodiment of the Beat Generation, because he served as the model for Dean Moriarty, the central character in the book that defined the Beat movement, Kerouac's *On the Road*.

Visions of Cody was not Kerouac's first attempt to document Cassady's life, and it would not be the last. Cassady appears, again as Cody Pomeray, in later works—*The Dharma Bums, Desolation Angels, Big Sur,* and *The Book of Dreams.*[10] In fact, much of Kerouac's career was dedicated to capturing Cassady in words, to trapping that elusive character within a definitive document that Kerouac would generate out of himself, "[t]elling the true story of the world in interior monolog." [11]

These repeated attempts to get at something like the "truth" of Neal Cassady suggest that Kerouac was never satisfied with

10. See Ann Charters, *Kerouac* (San Francisco: Straight Arrow, 1973), 410-11, for a complete index matching the real names with those used by Kerouac in various works.
11. Jack Kerouac, "Belief and Techniques for Modern Prose: List of Essentials," in Donald M. Allen and Robert Creeley, eds., *New American Story* (New York: Grove, 1965), 269. Hereafter cited as *NAS*.

the work he had done, that he recognized his own failure and even the inevitability of that failure. *Visions of Cody* exists because *On the Road* failed to capture Cassady, to pin him down, to transform him into a text. *Visions* even repeats whole scenes from the earlier novel, totally rewritten, as if Kerouac were trying again to tell the "true story" of those events, to get it right this time. Many of Kerouac's later works exist because *Visions of Cody* also failed. But Kerouac never gave up in his attempt to document Cassady. This documentation was, for him, something of a divine mission.

At the junction of the state line of Colorado, its arid western one, and the state line of Utah I saw in the clouds huge and massed above the fiery golden desert of eveningfall the great image of God with forefinger pointed straight at me through halos and rolls and gold folds that were like the existence of the gleaming spear in His right hand, and sayeth, Go thou across the ground; go moan for man; go moan, go groan, go groan alone go roll your bones, alone; go thou and be little beneath my sight; go thou, and be minute and as seed in the pod, but the pod the pit, world a Pod, universe a Pod; go thou, go thou, die hence; and of Cody report you well and truly. (*Cody,* 295)

Of course, there is no way of knowing how seriously we are to take all this, but Kerouac was serious enough about it to devote his career to documenting the life of Neal Cassady. And, in writing *Visions of Cody*, Kerouac faced the same question Mailer and Cantor also had to answer: How does one go about capturing the real in words?

Though *On the Road* does not have a coherent plot to hold the work together, it is structurally a traditional novel that accepts the rules of novelistic discourse — story, chronology, character, description, dialogue, etc. *Visions of Cody* begins within this discourse as well.

Around the poolhalls of Denver during World War II a strange
looking boy began to be noticable to the characters who frequented
the places afternoon and night and even to the casual visitors who
dropped in for a game of snookers after supper when all the tables
were busy in an atmosphere of smoke and great excitement and
a continual parade passed in the alley from the backdoor of one
poolroom on Glenarm Street to the backdoor of another—a boy
called Cody Pomeray, the son of a Larimer Street wino. (*Cody*, 47)

But very early on, Kerouac realizes that this traditional
novelistic discourse is not going to succeed in documenting
Cassady. *On the Road* was set within that same discourse, and
it failed—if it had not, there would have been no need to write
Visions of Cody. The documentation of Cassady's life begins
to assume gigantic proportions for Kerouac. It promises to
be an endless, infinite effort, exhaustive and exhausting in
its repetition. "My first great vision of Cody didn't come, as
I say, as I keep saying, as though I had to struggle to keep
saying, until 1948 . . ." (*Cody*, 295). It is a struggle to "keep
saying" the same thing over and over in the hope that, at some
point, Cassady himself as a human being, as a mystery, will
be exhausted in words and will disappear in favor of the text.

The problem is that Cassady/Pomeray—unlike Gilmore
and Guevara—is not a story with a beginning, a middle, and
an end. He is alive, always changing, shifting, capable at any
time of becoming something utterly different from what he
has always been. If Kerouac is to capture this continual flux,
if he is to hold fast in words that which cannot be held, he
needs a new strategy that will go beyond the novelistic discourse
which has already failed him.

And so, in *Visions of Cody*, Kerouac develops a kind of
writing designed to get to the "truth" that novelistic discourse
cannot seem to reach, a new writing that will capture the flow
of time. "Time being of the essence in the purity of speech,

sketching language is undisturbed flow from the mind of personal secret idea-words, *blowing* (as per jazz musician) on subject of image" (*NAS*, 270).

Kerouac proposes a kind of automatic writing, similar to that proposed by the Surrealists and later by William Butler Yeats. "If possible write 'without consciousness' in semi-trance (as Yeats' later 'trance writing') allowing subconscious to admit in own uninhibited interesting necessary and so 'modern' language what conscious art would censor, and write excitedly, swiftly, with writing-or-typing-cramps . . . (*NAS*, 271). The difference between the Surrealists and Yeats on the one hand and Kerouac on the other is that, while automatic writing proceeds *ex nihilo*, Kerouac wants to proceed "as per jazz musician" by improvising on a theme that preexists the performance. In *Visions of Cody*, that theme is Neal Cassady.

Kerouac's spontaneous prose method is an attempt to break through novelistic discourse while remaining inside it at the same time. Kerouac understands that traditional novelistic discourse cannot get at the truth because it excludes "what conscious art would censor." The forms of art dictate what can and cannot be said, and, for Kerouac, writing done within these forms is poetry. These forms will not accomplish what he wants, and so he writes, "No time for poetry but exactly what is" (*NAS*, 269).

His choice of words here is quite precise. If he is to accomplish an endless task, he certainly has no time for poetry. And, indeed, poetry is the discourse of "no time." Its forms, as Kerouac defines them, do not allow for the movement of time itself, and, in order to capture Neal Cassady in words, the author must capture that movement, for that constant flow and flux is "exactly what is."

Spontaneous prose is Kerouac's attempt to win a kind of authority for himself that traditional novelistic discourse denies him. The question of authority—of what it means to be an author — is extremely important for Kerouac, because he has good reason to doubt that the product of his authorship will get him where he wants to go. He has already failed to get at the truth of Cassady in *On the Road*, and throughout *Visions of Cody* he expresses serious doubts about what he is doing. Given the nature of his project, Kerouac cannot help poking fun at himself as author.

I had thought, in, and before college, that to be a writer was like being, of course, the Emile Zola of the film they made about him with Paul Muni shouting angrily in the streets at the dumb and stupid masses, as if he knew everything and they didn't know a damn thing; instead of that I wonder what working people think of me when they hear my typewriter clacking in the middle of the night or what they think I'm up to when I take walks at 2 A.M. in outlying suburban neighborhoods — the truth is I haven't a single thing to wr — feel foolish . . . (*Cody*, 259 — 60)

Kerouac would like to have the kind of authority that writers are supposed to have, that is, the authority granted to them by the culture at large. But he cannot gain that authority with respect to Neal Cassady, because, for one thing, he is not outside of Cassady's life, looking on with the supreme and quasi-scientific objectivity of a Zola — or of a Mailer. Kerouac is an intimate part of Cassady's story, which, of course, is not a story at all. And so, inevitably, as the one who documents Cassady, Kerouac finds himself slipping into the documentation again and again, reflecting on his assigned task, often apparently against his will. "I tried to write this at eleven it was called 'Mike Explores the Merrimack,' but now wait, I'm not supposed to enter into this but I guess I might as well . . ." (*Cody*, 267).

Kerouac enters his documentary text *as* documentarist again and again, because what he wants is the truth, and the truth is that he is part of this document and, at the same time, the one who writes it and who writes about the writing of it. As in Cantor's work on Guevara, this self-reflexivity allows Kerouac's text to mirror itself seemingly to infinity as it reflects and reflects again on its own reflections. The problem is, however, that even a potentially infinite text cannot seem to get to the real Neal Cassady who continues always to exist outside the book and who can even call the entire project into question. In one of his monologues transcribed from a tape recording, "Cody" encourages Jack to get stoned with him and adds: "Tell my story some other time. Put away your quills . . ." (*Cody*, 308). The telling of the story here is obviously secondary to real life, Cassady's real life, in the here and now.

In another taped monologue, "Cody" offers a stunning critique of the text itself and of the very effort of any documentary, of any attempt to get at the real through writing.

like if you tell me y — ah, or have gone through a thing completely in your own mind yourself, ah, and so that you've got it all formulated, and so that sometime a guy'll say "Hey, when's the first time you met Val?" well you say "Oh well I was walking down the street and that's how it happened," well, and so you say three or four times, so pretty soon, especially if it's a thought, not a happening, but a thought, so if you have to go through a thought again and again pretty soon it becomes an abstraction of the thought and you still follow the form and structure of it but you just say "Well so this happened and that happened," and it becomes just a dry, drab nothing, you see? It's not like it was at first. (*Cody*, 215 — 16)

Here, Cassady describes what Kerouac knows only too well — that the memory of what happened, the description of what happened, the writing of what happened, and the rewriting of what happened all falsify what indeed did happen, moving ever farther and farther from the event that was not description or memory or writing but a real happening. Inevitably, "it's not like it was at first."

Tape transcriptions like the above play an important part in *Visions of Cody*—in fact, one such transcription takes up almost 150 pages of the book. Because he doubts his own authority, Kerouac decides to trust to the authority of the objective tape recorder that simply records without judgment, without memory, without editing. Of course, Kerouac as author still had to transcribe what was said and add explanatory "stage directions," but his transcriptions are as close as possible to the original tapes. As in the above excerpt, Kerouac includes every "ah," "umm," and "well," every broken or partial phrase, every vocal sound. He leaves nothing out. As such, the transcripts are almost unreadable. But they are quite real, at least in theory.

In a 1968 interview, Kerouac casts doubt on this tape recorder method as a way of getting at the real. "I haven't used this method since; it really doesn't come out right, well, with Neal and with myself, when all written down and with all the Ahs and the Ohs and the Ahums and the fearful fact that the damn thing is turning and you're *forced* not to waste electricity or tape. . . ."[12]

Talking to a tape recorder is not the same as just talking, and so, for Kerouac, the tape recorder is not really an authority after all. But this was his opinion in 1968. In 1952, while he was writing *Visions of Cody*, the tape recording seemed to capture something of the real Neal Cassady, and so, following the section entitled "Frisco: The Tape," Kerouac includes a long section entitled "Imitation of the Tape." The idea here is, indeed, to become the recorder of his own flow of thoughts and sensations, to capture himself and Cassady much as the tape recorder did—directly, without judgment, distortion, or editing. The results?

12. "The Art of Fiction XLI: Interview with Jack Kerouac," *Paris Review* 11 (Summer 1968): 67-68.

just like Cody always says gar bless his old little ole hide that rin the thar rhide whoops whelap crack dhkeyr whoops aht the maggie and jiggs are running third aand fourth but there are indications that other things will soon aoccur by whih lookout she's coming back again where all liable to get killed around dhere and di fyou don't wash out an dkwhekek dhowowh but now I lost it again who wdra ahlow hdjo w drat it that I should have lost out again like happy old Yeaths now I saw one thing about yea y old Yeats and I say that he is a great man because he learned how to write oatutomatically at the behest of little (gragahest?) ghosts just like james mason wants it but I say and the only thing is you've got to explain yourself clearly or not at all. (*Cody*, 271)

Obviously, this "stream-of-typewriter" imitation of the tape does not allow Kerouac to explain himself clearly, nor does it get beyond the simple fact of language which is always itself and *not* Neal Cassady. Kerouac fails to reach the real Cody, and he knows it. What he wants is to record "the unspeakable visions of the individual" (*NAS*, 269), which, as unspeakable, are beyond the possibilities of recording.

Visions of Cody is, in a sense, a compendium of techniques — first-person narrative, third-person narrative, repetition, self-reflection, tape transcriptions, imitations of tape transcriptions, automatic writing, etc. — designed to shatter the discourse itself in favor of the real. But, of course, the text cannot stop being a text, cannot transcend its own textuality in favor of something beyond it. As Kerouac admits "we're getting to it indirectly and too late but completely from every angle except the angle we all don't know . . ." (*Cody*, 296).

The movement from Mailer's "true life novel" to Cantor's work to Kerouac's charts a gradual dissolution of novelistic discourse from within. For the most part, Mailer accepts a slightly altered form of traditional novelistic discourse as a means for getting at a reality that lies out there somewhere beyond the page. Cantor questions that discourse by questioning the authority of the author and the storiness of the story, creating a "truthful lie." In Kerouac's writing, the limits of novelistic discourse are assaulted so heroically and so relentlessly in the name of truth that, periodically, the text collapses into unreadable gibberish.

And yet, despite these attempts to alter or dissolve novelistic discourse per se, all three works are set firmly within that discursive realm insofar as each realizes — textually — the possibility of the impossible. Mailer's omniscience, Cantor's assumption of Guevara's voice, Kerouac's attempts to chronicle Neal Cassady from without and from within at the same time — all these strategies represent the impossible made real, but made real only on the printed page. Do these novels say something true about Gary Gilmore, Che Guevara or Neal Cassady? There is no way of knowing, for there is no objective standard — "what God saw" — by which they can be judged. If novelistic discourse is in fact the discursive realm in which impossibility is made possible, there still seems to be one impossibility that remains — the impossibility of novelistic discourse transcending itself in favor of a reality that, presumably, does not need words in order to be.

2

The Man in Buffalo:
Telling(,) the Teller(,) and the Told
in the Fiction of Raymond Federman

1.0: IT IS DAY. IT IS MIDNIGHT.

1.01: "There is no distinction between the real and the fictitious, the imaginary and the factual."

1.02: In the *Proslogium*, Saint Anselm addresses the question of the truth of discourse, of language. At one level, he conceives of truth as a correspondence between words and the state of the reality beyond words. This correspondence theory of truth, of course, is quite ancient and matches the common-sense view of what one means when one says that a statement is true. The sentence "it is day" is true if, in the world which exists independently of language, it is in fact daytime.

But for Saint Anselm there is another sense in which statements can be said to be true. He writes: "For, just as fire, when it warms, does the truth since it was determined by that from which it has its being, so also this sentence, *it is day*, does the truth when it signifies that it is day, whether it is day or not, since it was determined naturally to do that."

Here, Anselm is trying to account for the fact that a statement like "it is day" has meaning even when it does not correspond to the facts of extralinguistic reality. At night, the statement "it is day" is not true to these facts; it is a fiction, and yet it is true to itself.

There are two truths of language, then: the factive and the fictive. The distinction Anselm draws is clear. The factive statement "it is day" and the fictive statement "it is day" are true in very different ways and for very different reasons, even though the two sentences are identical word for word. It would seem that the factive and the fictive are separate realms of language. The factive points beyond itself; the fictive is self-contained.

And yet one must wonder why Anselm has applied the word "truth" to both linguistic realms, for if the factive and the fictive are equally true, then the distinction between them becomes confused.

Discourse is always true, even if it contradicts extralinguistic fact, even if it contradicts itself.

1:03: "In the fiction of the future, all distinctions between the real and the imaginary, between the conscious and the subconscious, between the past and the present, between truth and untruth will be abolished. All forms of duplicity will disappear. And, above all, all forms of duality will be negated. . . .

1.04: "But the truth is that fiction is not reality, it is simply a language which tells its own story, its own true story."

1.05: In the past decade, Raymond Federman has produced an impressive and innovative body of work, including the novels *Double or Nothing, Take It or Leave It, The Voice in the Closet, The Twofold Vibration,* and *Smiles on Washington Square* in English, as well as *Amer Eldorado* and *La voix dans le cabinet de debarras,* French drafts (but not translations) of *Take It or Leave It* and *The Voice in the Closet.* These are difficult works which call into question the very nature of fiction, fact, memory, language, and the author himself, and, because they offer a new kind of literary thought, they demand a new reading, an active reading, a reading that rewrites the texts in the process of its own activity.

Federman is also a well-known critic who has written often on innovative fiction and particularly on the works of the seminal figure in late twentieth-century literature, Samuel Beckett. His critical study *Journey to Chaos* is a definitive analysis of Beckett's early fiction, and, not surprisingly, Federman's studies of Beckett can serve as a key to his own challenging fictions.

1.06: "In my mind I have made of Beckett a kind of spiritual father. . . . I would almost say that everything I write is for Beckett, for his ultimate approval, which, of course, he will never give me, and must not give me."

1.07: In the closing passage of *Molloy,* Samuel Beckett's detective narrator Moran writes: "Then I went back into the house and wrote, It is midnight. The rain is beating on the windows. It was not midnight. It was not raining."

The statements "It is midnight. The rain is beating on the windows" are also the opening lines of part 2 of the novel in which Moran makes his report on his search for Molloy. In the first offering, there is nothing mysterious about these

sentences. The reader assumes the obvious: that Moran is sitting in his home, pen in hand, describing the state of reality
as it is at that moment. But in the repetition of these sentences,
there is a radical difference introduced into the reading. Here,
on the final page, "It is midnight. The rain is beating on the
windows" is a direct quotation, a rewriting in the present of
a past writing. "It was not midnight. It was not raining" would
seem to be a correction of that original statement, the admission of a past lie and the desire to tell the truth in the
present. With these sentences, Moran calls into question and
cancels all that has come before.

But Moran is not a person living in a world that could be
experienced without the intermediary of language. He is a
fictional character created by Samuel Beckett. Moran and
his world exist solely as words on paper, and neither he nor
that world have being beyond the words which describe them.

In what sense, then, is such a creature of language capable
of telling a lie or the truth?

1.08: Federman has commented on this passage from *Molloy*:

The paradoxical effect of this statement is, in fact, destroyed if one
recognizes that it is formulated on two different levels of rhetoric.
The affirmative part of the statement (in the present tense) corresponds to a fiction invented before our eyes by the narrator-hero
("I went back into the house and *wrote* . . ." he specifies), whereas
the negative part of the statement (in the past tense) merely points
to a reality which may or may not be true and, therefore, does not
necessarily relate to what is being written by Moran in the "report"
he claims he has been told to write.

1.09: There are several interesting points here. First, in his
explanation of Beckett's text Federman points out that a factive contradiction ("I wrote: It is midnight. . . . It was not

midnight") is not a contradiction in the fictive realm. Both statements can be true in the sense that they are true to themselves. There is no paradox, for each statement makes sense at its own level. It would seem, then, that fictional characters like Moran cannot lie, because, as Anselm has pointed out, words are always true, and Moran is both the producer and the product of words.

Second, Federman distinguishes two levels of (fictive) rhetoric. One is the fiction which exposes itself as fiction, "a fiction invented before our eyes." The other is the fiction which "points to a reality which may or may not be true" but which does not proclaim itself to be fact (the word "novel" still appears on the title page) nor confess itself as fiction by betraying the machinations of its fictivity.

1.10:   But if it is true that a character of fiction cannot lie, is it possible that the one whose name appears on the title page can and does? Does the fiction which exposes itself as fiction become fact? Is Federman's analysis as much a commentary on his own fiction as it is on Beckett's?

2.0:   THE TELLING IS ALSO TOLD

2.01:   "Fiction, in other words, need not agree with reality, especially when it is explicitly presented as subfiction — counterfeit inventions of the characters themselves."

2.02:   The above is Federman on Beckett's *Molloy*, but it is equally Federman on Federman, for his novels are such subfictions, inventions of fictive characters who often seem to be inventing each other as well, in a multiplicity of voices. *Double or Nothing*, for example, has four such voices, each presenting its own fictive truth. The first person, the recorder, writes the story of the second person, the writer, who is planning to write the story of the third person, a young man who arrives in America from France and begins to make his way here. The fourth person is introduced in a footnote:

It should be noted here that overlooking the whole intramural set up described in the preceding pages obviously there has to be a fourth person Someone to control organize supervise if you wish the activities and relations of the other three persons. . . . And therefore even though he may or may not be real and may never be heard and his presence never felt nonetheless is implied and implicit in the discourse. . . .

This fourth person would seem to be Federman himself, the creator of the other three characters, as Beckett is the creator of Moran. But this is not the case. Once the fourth person surfaces in the text, a fifth person is implied — that is, the person who records the existence of the fourth. The fifth person, of course, implies a sixth, and so on.

2.03: "Once you get involved in the so-called self-reflexive type of writing where the outside voice becomes part of the text, when the author himself becomes fictionalized, then you encounter an endless process. There is always another voice outside the text, a voice that precedes, supersedes each narrative voice, as in the drawing of the hand that holds the pen that draws itself. Obviously there is a real hand and a real pen that does the drawing and which can never be seen in the final drawing, however complicated and deceptive it becomes."

2.04: The texts and subtexts cannot reach some ultimate person who is the Author, Raymond Federman, for Federman is a fact. His name corresponds to a person who can be seen and heard and touched, who exists beyond words. The textual persons, however, are equal and only equal to themselves.

They do not transcend the words which constitute them. They are fictive.

3.0: SOMETHING OTHER THAN WHAT IS SAID

3.01: Is this true? In *Double or Nothing* and *Take It or Leave It*, the name "Raymond Federman" remains firmly in place on the title page; it does not enter the fictive text. In *The Twofold Vibration*, however, there is a Federman; or rather, the signifier "Federman" takes its place within the signifying field of the fiction. Within the context of the fiction, he is a recorder, the first-person narrator who sits at his typewriter and writes the story of another writer, the old man, as told to him by two intermediary narrators, Moinous and Namredef. He is the source of the fiction, but he is also an element within it. He is the source of the words and yet words himself.

Who is *this* Federman?

3.02: "Is what thinks in my place then another I?"

3.03: And who is *that* Federman?

That Raymond Federman, the one who exists independently of any text and who does not have to be read in order to be, was born in Paris and came to the United States shortly after World War II. His family was murdered in the Nazi camps, but young Raymond's parents saved their son by hiding him in a closet when the German soldiers came to their home. Federman lived in Detroit until 1951, when he was drafted and served in Asia until 1954. He studied at Columbia and UCLA, where he earned his MA and PhD. Since 1964, he has lectured as a faculty member of the State University of New York at Buffalo.

3.04: The above text is not equal to the Raymond Federman of *The Twofold Vibration* text, nor is it equal to the man named Raymond Federman who lives in Buffalo, New York. It is a language structure which is different from the text that constitutes the first Federman and which cannot limit and define the second Federman who exists beyond language. The second Federman cannot be captured in words; he is a fact. The first Federman is nothing more than what has been said of him; he is fiction.

But then who is the Raymond Federman who "was born in Paris. . . etc.?"

3.05: Who are these Federmen? What can be said about them?

3.06: Nothing can be said of the man who lives in Buffalo. He is beyond anything that might be said of him.

3.07: One can describe the events in the life of Raymond Federman who "was born in Paris. . . etc.," and this description is factive, for the words and the events correspond, or seem to. And yet, as Anselm has shown, the words offered above to define Federman (or those he might use to define himself) would be true even if Federman had not been born in Paris or come to the United States after World War II.

All possible Federmen are equally true as described, or equally fictive.

3.08: "It is day. It is midnight."

4.0: HE IS FEDERMAN, OR AT LEAST A FEDERMAN

4.01: It would be a mistake, then, to identify the Federmen of the novels or even the Federmen of critical studies, contributors' notes, or letters with the man who lives in Buffalo. The man in Buffalo is there. The other Federmen are textual beings, whether those texts be factive, fictive, or fa/ictive. To be, those characters must be read, for they are only as written.

4.02: Still there would seem to be obvious relationships between these textual Federmen, the other named and nameless characters who come into (textual) being through the novels, and the man who lives in Buffalo. For one thing, these textual beings exist only because, at some point in the past, the man in Buffalo wrote the words which constitute them. They are the traces of his activity, like the drips of paint on a canvas by Jackson Pollock.

But there are other relationships as well. There is good reason to believe that the man who lives in Buffalo was not born in the United States but immigrated here later in his life. At least he himself would seem to believe this, and there is enough supplementary evidence documenting his birth elsewhere and his later arrival here to allow for the conclusion that this, in fact, is what happened.

Curiously enough, the character sometimes known as Boris in *Double or Nothing* also was born in another country and came to America later, as did the writer in/of that novel. The same is true for the character Frenchy in *Take it or Leave it*, for Federman, Moinous, Namredef, and the old man in *The Twofold Vibration*, and for Moinous in *Smiles on Washington Square*.

4.03: In other words, the (textual) events of *Double or Nothing*, *Take it or Leave It*, *The Twofold Vibration*, and *Smiles on Washington Square* often (but not always) (seem to) correspond to (extratextual) events in the past life (and, therefore, in the present memory) of the man in Buffalo. Are these novels exercises in autobiography? What are the facts? Again, who is the man in Buffalo?

4.04: Nothing can be said of the man who lives in Buffalo. He is beyond anything that might be said of him.

4.05: "I am capable of becoming innumerable others, and I know that I shall forget this revelation once I am outside my own memory. This forgetting forms the object of my own limits."

5.0: THE SPEAKING I?

5.01: But has the man in Buffalo written the words which constitute these various textual Federmen and non-Federmen in order to re-create his own (extralinguistic) life in a linguistic form? Is he writing his memoirs in the guise of fiction, revealing and concealing the factive by way of the fictive?

5.02: "There is no writing which does not derive some means of protection, *to protect against* itself, against the writing by which the 'subject' is himself threatened as he lets himself be written: as he exposes himself."

5.03: By their own insistence, the man in Buffalo (the producer) and his (textual) subfiction writers (products/producers) do not write autobiography. Their writings are fictions, and the characters they create are different from themselves.

5.04: "But in case you guys get confused in the course of
                                            this
      twin recitation with the me and the he
         & the I and the He
         & the me now and the he then
         & the he past and the me present   (he past
                                        in the hole
                                        me present
                                        on the platform

let me make it quite clear once and for all lest WE
forget it
(here & there & everywhere)
I am here (alone)
He is there"

5.05: ". . . the guy whose story is now being told (second-hand) and whom you may sometime confuse with me, though I assure you was not me . . ."

5.06: "But in fact how can there be any truth in a second-hand recitation?"

5.07: By their own insistence, the man in Buffalo and his (textual) writers of subfictions are writing autobiography. Their writings are true, and they and the characters they create are equal.

5.08: "He is there (together we are)
As one are we not / multiple though single / I + HE
= WE or

We − I = HE pluralized in our singularity
me telling him
him telling me   etc."

5.09: Someone is lying.

5.10: "It is day. It is midnight."

5.11: Why are there always more questions than answers?

5.12: "there is nothing to question but the question itself"

5.13: Can a question be a lie?

5.14: "Words lie only for those who are haunted by the truth of words"

6.0: A REALITY WHICH MAY OR MAY NOT BE TRUE

6.01: If autobiography is possible at all, it is so because the writer's memories are accurate representations of completed past events and because he can represent those memories in language. Autobiography, then, is a representation of a representation, twice removed from extralinguistic experience.

6.02: Is memory always a truthful representation of the past?

6.03: "When I talk about my background, my youth, I'm never really sure if I am dealing with true facts or if I am in fact re-inventing what I think happened and who I was."

6.04: "The past is never finished, never completed; we can always go back to it."

6.05: Can language imitate memory?

6.06: "Language can but perfectly imitate language; more exactly, a discourse can but perfectly imitate a perfectly identical discourse. In short, a discourse can but imitate itself."

6.07: If language can only imitate itself, then it can imitate memory only if memory is language, that is, if memory of a (factive) event of the past is/becomes the (fictive) told of the present.

6.08: And yet the fictive events of the novels would seem to be similar to the remembered events of the life of the man in Buffalo. The voices of the fictions speak of moments which the voice of the man in Buffalo might also tell. Are these fictions, then, the answer to the question: Who is the man in Buffalo?

6.09: "after all let's be honest a biography or a guy's past experiences it's always something one invents afterwards in fact life is always a kind of fictional discourse a lot of bullshitting!"

7.0: VOICES TELLING AND TOLD

7.01: Who are these fictive voices, some named Federman, some nameless, some with names that change throughout the text? For the most part, they are the producers and the products of the fictive language. Of the four voices which constitute the *Double or Nothing* text, three are themselves producers of the subfictions that make up the total subfiction. The last person is the product of these multiple fictions.

The voice that is hidden behind the text, the fourth person, is the omniscient orchestrator of the fiction as a whole, though he himself is fictive insofar as he exists within the fiction he controls. His work, then, is a subfiction.

The first person, the recorder, also exists within the subfiction of the fourth person while he generates a subfiction of his own. This first person has no name, no story. Rather, he tells the story of the second person, also nameless, the writer who is preparing to write a fiction. This second person is the focal point of the work, for he stands between the realm of the factive and the fictive.

His problems (the second person, the inventor, the noodler) are, in a sense, double because he has to work out (mentally and physically) all the details of what he needs in the room (within the limits of his rather limited means), and at the same time invent, or at least organize in one way or another, the details of what he is going to write once he has locked himself in the room. . . .

He plans to get a room, supply it with all that he will need to stay there for a year (noodles, toothpaste, toilet paper, coffee, cigarettes, etc.), and use that time to write his novel. *Double or Nothing* is his story, a collection of lists, calculations, and thoughts about what he will need in his room as well as notes for his soon-to-be-written fiction. This writer (and his first-person voice) must act on two levels at once: the factive (i.e., the physical necessities, the noodles, the toothpaste, etc.) and the fictive (the story he is planning to write).

7.02: "One learns to live a double life while writing, not only double but simultaneous lives."

7.03: "it's all an illusion a fiction a lie the only truth now is the NOODLES"

7.04: And yet this is not quite correct, for there really are no factive elements in the writer's life. His room, his noodles, and the notes for his novel (the factive and the fictive) are products of the subfiction produced by the first-person recorder, as is the writer himself. The facts of his life are only apparent. For the writer, as for Saint Anselm, the realms of the factive and fictive collapse into each other.

7.05: "It is day. It is midnight."

7.06: And who is the third person of *Double or Nothing*, the immigrant who arrives in America from France? The writer (second person) suggests that this third person's story is factive, that it was told to him by a real individual, that it actually happened, though he tries to hide this truth by refusing to use the young man's real name and by calling him Jacques, Robert, Boris, etc., at various points in the narrative. On the other hand, the writer (second person) also insists that Boris' story is not true, that the character and his tale are products of the imagination, of the (as yet unwritten) subfiction. He writes:

> they'll think I am talking about myself all the time
> whereas
> in fact
> this is not so   I insist on this point
>   I am inventing most of this

7.07:   But then who is Boris, etc.? He is the text which defines him, a text which may or may not be true to events in the world beyond language but which is clearly true to itself, even when it contradicts itself, as Anselm's definition of linguistic truth demonstrates. The Boris-text, then, is true, whether it is wholly factive, wholly fictive, or fa/ictive.

And yet the writer (second person) seems to feel that Boris, even a fictive Boris, exists beyond the printed page. "But at this stage BORIS starts an argument with me because he does not like what I am doing to ERNEST. But since I have a great advantage over BORIS as his progenitor. Since I literally control his existence. If for some reason he argues with me and I find I do not like what he says to me I destroy him." A disagreement between character and author (between fictive and factive) seems incredible, but in *Double or Nothing* it is clearly possible, for at this level character and author are both textual products. As beings who depend on a fictive narrative for their existence, the character and the author, the product and the producer, are equals.

Are these equals perhaps identical? Is the present story of the third person equal to the past, the memory of the second? The writer (not the man in Buffalo) suggests that this is the case. "And so, having decided that Boris would spend the rest of his life in America, there was nothing else to do but go on and on to the end, especially since eventually he too would lock himself in a room with noodles to crap out his existence on paper. . . ." Pushing this idea a bit farther, is the present of the second person the past of the first, and is his present the past of the fourth, etc.? Are these four voices one? And is this composite person the past life of the man who lives in Buffalo?

7.08: Someone (who?) suggests that first, second, third fourth, etc., are one.
    me you I he all of us together

7.09: Someone (who?) suggests that they are not.
    It's my story . . . NO . . . it's his story . . . HIS only HIS

7.10: Who is right? Who is who?

7.11: Who is the man in Buffalo?

7.12: Nothing can be said of the man who lives in Buffalo. He is beyond anything that might be said of him.

8.0: EVERY STORY IS THE STORY OF ANOTHER

8.01: The text of *Double or Nothing* brings us no closer to the man whose name appears on the title page of the work (presumably the author, the man in Buffalo). There is no *Double or Nothing* beyond the text which constitutes *Double or Nothing*, and there are no persons or stories or facts beyond that text. The pages of the fiction are what they are, and there is no relationship between the words printed there and the persons and events in the world beyond words, except for the fact that these traces themselves, the pages, and the book are objects in that world beyond language. That is . . .

8.02: Who is the man in Buffalo?

8.03: *Double or Nothing* is not the answer to this question.

8.04: "Fiction, in other words, need not agree with reality."

9.0: THE PRODUCT AND THE PRODUCER(S)

9.01: *Take It or Leave It* is also the product of many voices telling and told by each other. This text is an "exaggerated second-hand tale," according to the note on the title page, which, at the outset, places the work at two removes from what we might want to think of as the reality beyond words. A tale is not an event in the extratextual world, and an exaggerated second-hand tale lacks even the questionable accuracy and immediacy of an eye-witness account. Here, the secondary teller must remember and put into words the remembering and the putting-into-words of the original teller (now the told), and so the tale itself is immediately suspect and open to error throughout.

9.02: The tale: A young French immigrant who came to America after the death of his family during World War II is drafted into the U.S. Army and requests a transfer to the

Korean theater to get out of the 82nd Airborne Division. The transfer comes through, and Frenchy has thirty days to get from Fort Bragg, North Carolina, to California where he will meet his ship. He decides to go by car, in his own Buick Special, and see America, but because of a bureaucratic error his papers and the money he needs to make his trip are sent off to Camp Drum in upstate New York. He must get there himself, make the drive from North Carolina to New York before he can begin his journey west.

9.03: The teller: The tale, full of false starts, digressions, repetitions, and contradictions, is told by a nameless (?) voice that is addressing a faceless and almost voiceless audience. The teller and Frenchy (the told) have much in common, so much in fact that one is tempted to think of them as the same person, though, for the most part, the teller insists that they are not ("I'm only a second-hand teller" "The guy . . . you may sometime confuse with me, though I assure you was not me, but whom I sometime try to make myself pass for").

The teller, then, tells a tale that is not his own but one that was told to him (presumably) by Frenchy (though perhaps not) while they sat together under a tree or at the edge of a precipice or somewhere else.

There are no admitted fictions here, like the novel about Boris projected by the writer (not the man in Buffalo) of/in *Double or Nothing*. And yet there are also no truths here, no events. Again, there are only words.

9.04: There are other voices as well. Though the listeners in the audience do not speak intelligibly ("BLAH, BLAH, BLAH . . . ? PISTT, PISTT, PISTT . . . ?"), the teller understands their questions, comments, and interruptions and tries his best to respond to them ("DAMMIT WILL YOU

GUYS STOP BUGGING ME WITH YOUR FUCKING QUESTIONS"). There are literary critics-in-residence in the text (Claude, Cam Taathaam) who comment on the very work which gives them their being. And there are others.

Still, Frenchy and the teller are the focal point(s) of the text. Frenchy, the original teller of the tale, is the told of *Take It or Leave It*. But the teller is told as well. Without *Take It or Leave It*, he would not and could not exist. Like the voices of *Double or Nothing*, the teller is both producer and product of the text.

9.05: And who tells the teller?

9.06: Who dictates these words, who forces them into the narrator's mouth?

9.07: The name "Raymond Federman" appears on the title page, though not in the text itself. Is this Federman the teller of the teller? Or is he in turn told by another, by the one (perhaps the man in Buffalo) who inscribed the name beneath the title of the book?

9.08: Is Federman perhaps the teller of the text, relating in disguise the events of his own life? Is he the speaking I? Is he teller and told? Is he the man in Buffalo? What is true here?

9.09: "It is day. It is midnight."

9.10: "But in fact how can there be any truth in a second-hand recitation?" And how can there be a recitation which is not second (third fourth fifth nth)-hand?

10.0: WORDS AND YET WORDS

10.01: Like *Double or Nothing, Take It or Leave It* is a text which constitutes, contradicts, and erases itself, as it constitutes, contradicts, and erases the voices which it produces and by which it is produced. The reading of the text leaves no remainder. In canceling itself, the novel refuses to serve as the story of Frenchy, the teller, Federman (of the title page), or the man in Buffalo, if "story" is a coherent sequence of (actual) (remembered) (imagined) events. It is, rather, the sum of its own words, each of which is a material reality. *Take It or Leave It* is fiction, as all words are fictive, and truth as all words are true.

10.02: "The distinction between truth and untruth, fact and fiction, becomes irrelevant."

10.03: There is every reason to believe that the man in Buffalo did the actual work that produced *Take It or Leave It*. In what sense, then, is it *his* text? There are striking similarities between the (actual) (reported) (remembered) events of his life and the (textual) events of the novel, and yet there is also a striking difference. The man in Buffalo is not language, and the (past) (present) (future) events of his life are not words. *Take It or Leave It* is language and only language.

10.04: *Double or Nothing* and *Take It or Leave It* are texts, texts are facts, and the writing or the reading of a text is an event. But the textual events of/in these works are not extra-linguistic facts or events. They are repetitions of other texts and pre-texts, perhaps imagined or remembered by the man in Buffalo, perhaps written by him or by others.

Though there are similarities between the textual events in/of *Double or Nothing* and *Take It or Leave It* and the (reported) events in the past life of the man in Buffalo, still these works are not exercises in autobiography. In fact, they are precisely the opposite of autobiographical (factive) texts, for they are purposefully and obviously fictive, and their fictivity is betrayed at every step. The digressions, the self-reflections, the contradictions, and the false starts belie the storiness of the story time and again. These texts are lies which confess their falsehood.

10.05: And yet isn't a lie that betrays itself the truth?

10.06: "I'm always suspicious of the kind of fiction that pretends to tell the truth. I don't know what truth is, but I know that maybe out of a series of lies that deny themselves, one may reach a kind of truth. In other words, I use the word lie, the lie of fiction, in the sense of the paradox of fiction."

10.07: What is the truth about the man in Buffalo?

10.08: Who is the man in Buffalo? *Double or Nothing* and *Take It or Leave It* can tell us very little about him, for he is not equal to these texts and they are not equal to him. Much is said here, but the man in Buffalo is always something else, something other than what is said.

10.09: "Every story is the story of another."

10.10: "all stories are the same"

10.11: But is the man in Buffalo also something other than the saying?

11.0: THE F(f)EDERMAN OF TITLE PAGE AND TEXT

11.01: *The Twofold Vibration* and *The Voice in the Closet* mark a turning point in the writings of the man in Buffalo and in this interrogation of those writings and of him. Again, the name "Raymond Federman" appears on the title page, but, for the first time, the name also appears in the fictions themselves. Federman joins Boris, Frenchy, and the others in the contexts of the texts; the name becomes purposefully fictive.

11.02: What has become of the man in Buffalo whose name, by all accounts, is also Raymond Federman?

11.03: In *The Twofold Vibration*, Federman is a character and the speaking I, but he is not alone. He shares the narrative voice with two others: Namredef (his mirror image) and Moinous (me/we). Together, they (the tellers) tell the story of their friend the old man (the told) who, like his three tellers and like the man in Buffalo, is a bilingual French immigrant and a survivor of the Holocaust. He is also a writer, a producer of (sub)fictions and the product of *The Twofold Vibration*.

11.04: The old man's story is a not-yet, a tale out of time (the subtitle for *The Twofold Vibration* is "an extemporaneous novel"). It is almost midnight ("it was not midnight"), December 31, 1999, and, at the coming of the millennium, the old man is to be deported from earth to the space colonies. His friends are trying to find out why he is being deported and to save him if possible. They are also trying to tell his story ("the real story, no more evasions"), and in the process, they digress into his past (?) and tell about his affair with actress June Fanon, his spectacular win at the Travemunde Casino, his literary efforts, etc. They are trying to say their unnamed friend completely, usually by repeating what he has said about himself, and in the attempt they also say themselves. But the who and the why of the old man continually escape them, as the old man seems continually to escape himself and his own story.

11.05: Namredef and Moinous are the investigators, and Federman is the recorder, the orchestrator of the text. This Federman sits in his room at his desk and records the reports, observations, and reminiscences of Moinous and Namredef, making his own contributions along the way. He is the explainer, the fictioneer, the teller of the tellings of his two co-narrators. He is the one who does the physical work which creates the material text.

He is Federman, or at least a Federman. Is he, then, the man who lives in Buffalo?

11.06: The Federman of *The Twofold Vibration* is the teller of the old man, Namredef, and Moinous, but he in turn is told by another, by the Raymond Federman of the title page, by the man in Buffalo. The text implies the man in Buffalo, but neither it nor its voices are equal to him. He is not in/of *The Twofold Vibration*. The man in Buffalo is not equal to Federman or Moinous or Namredef or the old man, those who do not and cannot exist beyond the text. These others are complete as written. But, for the man in Buffalo, there can always be more words.

12.0: A FICTION INVENTED BEFORE OUR EYES

12.01: In the context of *The Voice in the Closet*, form is crucial and incredibly strict: twenty pages, eighteen lines per page, sixty-eight characters (letters and spaces) per line; the text is a series of perfectly justified boxes that take on the shape of the closet itself. Within that form, only the essential can remain. There is no room for a story, only a voice speaking from within the boxes of words.

12.02: In the bilingual edition of *The Voice in the Closet* published in 1979 (which also includes "Echos à Raymond Federman," Maurice Roche's unique response to the *Voice* texts), both the English and the French versions are the work of the man whose name appears on the title page: Raymond Federman. But there is another federman here, lodged (trapped) (enclosed) in the text itself. Who is this federman?

He (federman) is not the voice in the closet, though there is a voice, the voice of a boy (a fictive character) speaking within the fiction in the first person ("in my own voice at last a beginning") to someone named federman, the writer who tells him ("his fingers on the machine make me") but who has failed again and again to tell the truth about him and his life ("never getting it straight his repetitions").

The boy's parents have hidden him in the closet of their home, and, while he crouches there in the darkness, he hears German troops taking his mother, his father, and his two sisters away to die in the camps. He waits, but no one comes for him. For some reason, or for no reason at all, the boy has survived. The writer, federman, has tried to tell the story of the boy often ("take it or leave it . . . double or nothing"), to get at the meaning of that survival ("my survival a mistake he cannot accept"), but he has only repeated himself endlessly ("plagiarizing my life"), losing track of the tale in the telling of it. He has never found the words he needs. The boy ("born voiceless") has waited for a long time for federman to tell the story completely; now he knows that he must tell it himself, create the truth of himself in words. The told becomes the teller, the voice.

The voice wants to tell the truth, to "abolish his sustaining paradox expose the implausibility of his fiction," but, like federman, the boy also fails to find the proper beginning for a story that is terrible beyond words. There is no truth here. *The Voice in the Closet* remains fiction. The voice cancels itself and its author.

12.03: The Federman in *The Twofold Vibration* and the federman in *The Voice in the Closet* are not the same person. Federman is the teller of the old man, of Moinous, and of Namredef, but he in turn is told by/within the text of *The Twofold Vibration*. In *The Voice in the Closet*, on the other hand, federman is the former teller ("a story teller told"), now told by the boy and by the author of the text. But are either of these F(f)edermen equal to the third Raymond Federman whose name appears on the title page?

And what can these F(f)edermen tell us about the man in Buffalo?

12.04: "I is author, user of words, integral, multiple, familiar to itself, and stranger. It is subject and object, it is the shape of itself in print."

12.05: "The I that writes the text is never, itself, anything more than a paper I."

12.06: The voice tells federman and itself. But the federman at the typewriter also tells the voice and himself. And federman and the voice are also told. By the Raymond Federman of the title page? By the man in Buffalo?

12.07: "But if I am named, I name in turn."

12.08: Who is the man in Buffalo?
Check one: ( ) Boris   ( ) Frenchy   ( ) Moinous
            ( ) Namredef   ( ) Raymond Federman
            ( ) Federman   ( ) federman
            ( ) the voice in the closet
            ( ) all of the above
            ( ) other [specify] _____

12.09: "By now the name federman has become a symbol in the text."

12.10: "It would seem that the author's name, unlike other proper names, does not pass from the interior of a discourse to the real and exterior individual who produced it; instead, the name seems always to be present, marking off the edges of the text, revealing, or at least characterizing, its mode of being."

12.11: Who is the man in Buffalo? *Double or Nothing, Take It or Leave It, The Twofold Vibration,* and *The Voice in the Closet* can tell us very little about him, for he is not equal to these texts and they are not equal to him. Much is said here, but the man in Buffalo is always something else, something other than what is said.

13.0: REMEMBER AND PUT INTO WORDS THE REMEMBERING AND THE PUTTING-INTO-WORDS

13.01: What is it that the man in Buffalo is trying to say?

13.02: He is trying to say saying, trying to create texts that do not conceal themselves but maintain and make evident their own textuality. He is trying to write texts that are about nothing, texts that do not point beyond the printed page. He is trying to write writing, a writing that is both process and product, a writing that is fictive (see 1.02).

13.03: "I don't want you to read me just for my story, but mostly for the language, because, ultimately, that's all we *are*, that's what keeps us together, language."

13.04: The man in Buffalo is also trying to say himself, to come to terms with his own experience, or rather with his memory of that experience. He is trying to say the vital moments of his life that, as lived moments, were not said. He is trying to write his own time, including the time of the writing itself. He is trying to write a writing that is factive (see 1.02).

13.05: "life is but a fiction"

13.06: The man in Buffalo is failing. His writing can neither be equal to nor avoid his time. He is out(side) of words. His verbal facts are fictive, but his fictions are facts.

   He cannot not fail.

13.07: "Once you commit yourself to a piece of paper you're committing yourself to failure."

13.08: "It is day. It is midnight."

13.09: "one truth is as good as another"

13.10: Who is the man in Buffalo? Like the voices of the novels, he is the producer and the product of his texts, the teller and the told. He is the subject of the texts and subject to them. He is the sum of his (past, present, and future) texts and the texts of others (past, present, and future). He is all of these.

13.11: And yet he is always something else.

13.12: "One must write in order to have a name. One must be called something."

13.13: "The deed as well as the doer are fictions."

Sources

Anselm. "Dialogue on Truth." In Richard McKeon, ed., *Selections from Medieval Philosophy.* New York: Scribners', 1957. 1:150–84

Barthes, Roland. "From Work to Text." In Josué V. Harari, ed., *Textual Strategies: Perspectives in Post-Structuralist Criticism,* 73–81. Ithaca: Cornell University Press, 1979.

Derrida, Jacques. *Writing and Difference.* Trans. Alan Bass. Chicago: University of Chicago Press, 1978.

Everman, Welch D. "Who?" *Small Press Review* 7 (November-December 1975): 3.

Federman, Raymond. *Double or Nothing.* Chicago: Swallow Press, 1971.

———. "Surfiction—Four Propositions in Form of an Introduction." In Raymond Federman, ed., *Surfiction: Fiction Now and Tomorrow,* 5–15. Chicago: Swallow Press, 1975.

———. *Take It or Leave It.* New York: Fiction Collective, 1976.

———. *The Voice in the Closet.* Madison: Coda Press, 1979.

———. *The Twofold Vibration.* Bloomington: Indiana University Press, 1982.

———. *Smiles on Washington Square.* New York: Thunder's Mouth Press, 1986.

Foucault, Michel. "What is an Author?" In Harari, *Textual Strategies,* 141—60.

Genette, Gerard. "Boundaries of Narrative." Trans. Ann Levonas. *New Literary History* 8 (1976): 1—13.

Klossowski, Pierre. "Nietzsche's Experience of the Eternal Return." Trans. Allen Weiss. In David B. Allison, ed., *The New Nietzsche: Contemporary Styles of Interpretation,* 106—37. New York: Dell, 1977.

Lacan, Jacques. "The Insistence of the Letter in the Unconscious." Trans. Jan Miel, In Jacques Ehrmann, ed., *Structuralism,* 101—37. Garden City: Doubleday Anchor, 1970.

McCaffery, Larry. "A Real Fictitious Interview with Raymond Federman." Manuscript in possession of the author.

Nietzsche, Friedrich. *The Will to Power.* Trans. Walter Kaufmann and R. J. Hollingdale. New York: Vintage, 1968.

Sartre, Jean-Paul. *Saint Genet.* Trans. Bernard Frechtman. New York: New American Library, 1964.

Part Two
The Authority of The Discourse

3

Harry Mathews'
Selected Declarations of Dependence:
Proverbs and the Forms of Authority

TO SPEAK OR TO WRITE is always to perform within the confines of a language that is given, a language that preexists every act of speaking and writing, every speaker and writer. To use language, then, is to accept its limits, its vocabulary, its rules, and to express oneself, to make one's own statement, in a medium that is not one's own, that one did not create but found already intact. It is, in a very real sense, language that speaks or writes in the place of the speaker or writer who is always already caught up within that language. Jacques Lacan has suggested that every subject comes into the realm of language, within this arena of otherness, simply by being born. "The speaking subject, if he seems to be thus a slave of language, is all the more so of a discourse in the universal moment of which he finds himself at birth, even if only by dint of his proper name." [1]

If this is so, if every linguistic performance is a function of language as such, if, according to Michel Foucault, writing is "an interplay of signs, regulated less by the content it signifies than by the very nature of the signifier," [2] then the concept of the author — the one who wields authority as a user of language, the one who masters language and expresses himself or herself through that mastery — becomes open to question.

As a writer, as a literary artist, Harry Mathews has posed the question of the author directly: "Every writer who confronts a world without meaning and undertakes to transform it through language must answer the questions: Where do I begin? What right have I to speak at all?" [3]

Mathews' questions go beyond the issue of authority to address the very subjectivity of the author, the self that is to be expressed in the act of writing. If, as Lacan suggests, the subject is always already a function of a language that is itself always the language of the other, then who or what is this self that is expressed in writing? It would seem that to write — to assume the author's place — is not to assume or even to seize authority but, paradoxically, in the very moment of writing to abdicate it, and to attempt to express the self in writing is to submit irrevocably to the place of the other.

Harry Mathews understands and accepts language as the realm within which he must perform. In fact, as Mathews

1. Jacques Lacan, "The Insistence of the Letter in the Unconscious," trans. Jan Miel, in Jacques Ehrmann, ed., *Structuralism* (Garden City: Doubleday, 1970), 104.

2. Michel Foucault, *Language, Counter-Memory, Practice,* trans, Donald F. Bouchard and Sherry Simon (Ithaca: Cornell University Press, 1977), 116.

3. Harry Mathews, "Georges Perec," *Grand Street* 3 (Autumn 1983): 143.

also knows, literary discourse — his specific arena of performance — is far more limited and limiting than language as such. Novelistic discourse, poetic discourse, dramatic discourse, are highly restricted areas within language, each with its own set of rules which establish the boundaries of the genre. Literature *is* the creation of limited arenas within language as such, and every literary work takes place within such an arena. According to the late Italo Calvino, "Literature is a combinatorial game which plays on the possibilities intrinsic to its own material, independently of the personality of the author."[4]

Calvino suggests here that the literary writer's role is not that of author but of medium and that the literary work is, in essence, a working out of combinations and permutations of given elements, a "working out" which has nothing to do with the writer as subject. Such thinking is rooted in the theories of OuLiPo (Ouvroir de Litterature Potentielle), the French group of experimental writers, philosophers, and mathematicians brought together by Raymond Queneau and François Le Lionnais in 1960, a group that has included among its members not only Calvino but Georges Perec, Marcel Benabou, Jean Lescure, and, of course, Harry Mathews. Indeed, it would be impossible to overestimate the influence Mathews' own membership in OuLiPo has had on his work. To understand his orientation toward writing, it is important to understand what OuLiPo is all about.

OuLiPo is dedicated to the exploration of "constrictive forms" in literature — in Calvino's terms, literary games with highly determined rules. Mathews defines the constrictive forms of the OuLiPo as "procedures and structures so peremp-

---

4. Italo Calvino, "Myth in the Narrative," trans. Erica Freiberg, in Raymond Federman, ed., *Surfiction: Fiction Now and Tomorrow* (Chicago: Swallow Press, 1975), 79.

tory in their demands that no one using them can avoid subordinating his personal predilections to them" (140). Like Calvino, Mathews is defining an orientation toward writing that transcends the subjectivity and the supposed authority of the one who writes. Within the boundaries established by a constrictive form, authority is rooted in the form itself, in the discourse defined and generated by that form. By working within a constrictive form, by abdicating any claim to self and authority, the writer transcends himself or herself in favor of writing per se. As Mathews says: "There is no value inherent in the product of a constrictive form, except one: being unable to say what you normally would, you must say what you normally wouldn't."[5] In other words, to write within a constrictive form, you must give up your claim to self-expression, your claim to be you.

The forms developed or rediscovered by members of the OuLiPo group are often almost unbelievably constrictive, and of course the more constrictive they are, the more the writer must submit to the authority of the forms themselves. Many of these forms have been explored before — by the Grands Rhetoriqueurs of the fifteenth and sixteenth centuries, among others.[6] Many are the invention of OuLiPo members. For example, Queneau's *100,000 Billion Poems* is based on his own elaborate system of constraints outlined in his essay "Cent mille milliards de poemes. Mode d'emploi."[7] The completed work

5. Harry Mathews, "Vanishing Point," in Richard Kostelanetz, ed., *The Avante-Garde Tradition in Literature* (Buffalo: Prometheus Books, 1982), 312. Hereafter cited as "Vanishing Point."

6. Warren F. Motte, Jr., *The Poetics of Experiment: A Study of the Work of Georges Perec* (Lexington, Ky.: French Forum, 1984), 19.

7. Raymond Queneau, *Cent mille milliards de poémes* (Paris: Gallimard, 1961); Raymond Queneau, "Cent mille milliards de poémes. Mode d'emploi," in OuLiPo, *La litterature potentielle: Creations Re-creations Recreations* (Paris: Gallimard, 1973), 247-49.

is a collection of ten sonnets. The sonnet, of course, is a constrictive form in its own right. But under Queneau's system,
the first lines of all ten sonnets are interchangeable. So are
all ten second lines, all ten third lines, and so on. Each sonnet in the book is printed on a right-hand page, and each
page is sliced into fourteen strips, one per line of poetry. By
flipping these strips back and forth, by combining, say, the
first line of the first poem, the second line of the ninth, the
third line of the fifth, etc., the reader can construct his own
perfect sonnet — one Queneau not only did not write (in a
traditional, authorial sense) but one which he probably never
even imagined, since this is only one of 100,000 billion
possibilities in the book. Queneau's constrictive system gives
rise to a work that no author could possibly write — even a
poet who could crank out a sonnet a minute, twenty-four hours
a day, seven days a week could produce only something in
the neighborhood of half a million sonnets a year — a frac-
tion of the total number of sonnets in Queneau's book. *100,000
Billion Poems* is a book that could only write itself.

Palindromes and lipograms are ancient forms that the
OuLiPo has rediscovered. A palindrome, of course, is a word,
phrase, or sentence that reads the same backward as
forward — say, "radar" or "Madam, I'm Adam." Working in
this form, OuLiPo member Georges Perec composed a palindrome of more than 5,000 letters — a work the length of a short
story — that, amazingly, is about the palindrome, about the
very form that generates the text.[8]

A lipogram is any text that purposely does not make use
of one or more letters of the alphabet.[9] Obviously, some
lipograms (say, one that omits the letter *x)* are less difficult

8. Georges Perec, "Palindrome," in OuLiPo, *La litterature,* 101–6.
9. Georges Perec, "Histoire du lipogramme," in OuLiPo, *La litterature,*
77–93.

than others (say, one that omits a vowel). Of course, the members of OuLiPo have faced the lipogram in its most constrictive forms.

Queneau has written a short lipogram omitting the letter *e* (the most commonly used letter in French, as in English) and another that avoids *e, a,* and *z*.[10] But Georges Perec carries the lipogram to its logical extreme in his novel *La disparition*, which is a book-length lipogram in *e* that takes its very shape from the absent letter.[11] As Mathews explains:

Without e, what has become unspeakable and what remains to be said? Perec's genius was to make this question the subject of his fiction; to make it his fiction. . . . In Oulipian terms, he transformed a syntactic construction into a semantic one. . . . By the end of *La Disparition,* e has become whatever is unspoken or cannot be spoken—the unconscious, the reality outside the written work that determines it and that it can neither escape nor master. E has become what animates the writing of fiction; it is the fiction of fiction. ("Vanishing Point," 312−13)

OuLiPo members—Mathews among them—have made use of many other constrictive forms, some old, some new, some relatively simple, some based on elaborate mathematical formulae. But what is the point here? What is the relationship, if any, between these experiments and the possibilities of writing, particularly literary writing?

At one level, the OuLiPo experiments are simply that—experiments with no particular ends in sight. As Mathews has made clear, OuLiPo is not a literary school in any real sense.

10. Raymond Queneau, "Lipogramme en e" and "Lipogramme en a, en e, et en z," in OuLiPo, *La litterature,* 97-98.
11. Georges Perec, *La disparition,* (Paris: Denoel, 1969).

It produces no literary works; it does not claim that constrictive structures are the writer's salvation. It proposes such structures only for the sake of their *potentiality*. The name of the group means "workshop of potential literature," but an *ouvroir* was also a place where devoted ladies gathered to knit woolens for the needy. In isolating new or neglected structures in experimental conditions, the Oulipo's aim is to provide methods that writers can use according to their needs. To the Oulipo, the value of a structure is its ability to produce results, not the quality of those results, which will be demonstrated elsewhere, if at all. The most the Oulipo ever does is supply one or a few examples of each structure, to show that it works. These examples are intentionally "frivolous": they are meant to avoid prejudicing the structure's future yield; no one should be able to mistake them for models. ("Vanishing Point," 311–12)

But even if the OuLiPo experiments are not literary works in themselves, it seems that they can give rise to literary works like *100,000 Billion Poems, La disparition*, and the writings of Harry Mathews—novels like *The Conversions, Tlooth,* and *The Sinking of the Odradek Stadium*, stories like those collected in *Country Cooking*, or the poems in *Trial Impressions*. But what is the difference between a "frivolous" experiment with words and a literary work based on a constrictive form? Mathews suggests an answer to this question in his discussion of Perec's *La disparition*—while the frivolous experiment merely plays itself out according to the strictures of the form, the *literary* work based on a constrictive form draws its very meaning from the form itself by pushing the discourse allowed within the form to its logical extreme. In a very real sense, such a work confirms the authority of the form and transcends it at the same time. Paradoxically, it would seem that the text which owes most to the authority of a particular restricted discourse is also the text that does most to transform and to extend that discourse, to force it to go beyond itself, to say what it has not said before.

Harry Mathews has devoted his career to writing literary texts within such forms, submitting to them while at the same time forcing them to speak at their own boundaries. *Selected Declarations of Dependence* is a collection of such texts, based on various combinations of a very limited number of elements — a restricted vocabulary drawn from a very particular discourse.

The source of Mathews' declarations is the proverb, that commonplace bit of conventional wisdom which seems to belong to no one and everyone. Proverbs are cultural clichés, secondhand language. In a sense, of course, all language is secondhand, but the proverb is a special case, because it is also pre-packaged. As a cliché, the proverb is a phrase or sentence that functions as a unit, as a sign in its own right, a sign that everyone understands immediately, without the need for thought or interpretation. It is unmediated language, perfect language, dead language. In Mathews' words: "The Other makes words dead, to teach things dead."[12]

But, of course, the proverb is a very special kind of cliché, for it bears within itself a formidable authority. Proverbs offer advice, but to use a proverb is not to speak with one's own limited authority. It is to speak with the authority of the entire culture which has adopted the proverb as an expression of its collective wisdom. It is to speak not with one's own voice but with the voice of the They, for a proverb is what They say. They say: Once bitten, twice shy. They say: A stitch in time saves nine. To quote a proverb is to speak without speaking, to speak with the voice of the other, to speak and yet to give up any claim of authority for what one says. It is to claim and to disclaim at the same time.

12. Harry Mathews, *Selected Declarations of Dependence* (Calais: Z Press, 1977), 4. Hereafter cited in text.

Mathews' explorations in *Selected Declarations of Dependence* are designed to maintain the discourse of proverbs but at the same time to undermine their collective authority by carefully dismantling them, perhaps in hopes of making them say something new. "Words are gathered," Mathews writes, "not made, for intentions new and old: other men's words, all men's words. Will a few old words propose new intentions?" (2).

Mathews proposes his new intentions by creating strict rules for the writing of his texts. He selects forty-six proverbs which provide a vocabulary of some 185 words, and with this vocabulary he writes "Their Words, For You," a love story. The method of composition is made clear in "Forty-Six Proverbs and Their Uses," an introduction which explains the rules of *Selected Declarations of Dependence* and which, at the same time, adheres to those rules: "And for the words that are, for you, at hand, the renderings were broken down into words taken one at a time" (4).

"Their Words, For You" is, indeed, a story built from the fragments of dismantled proverbs, and yet the words come together again and again in proverbial structures. The text generates many new proverbs, constructed from bits of old proverbs and sharing their traditional form but without their built-in authority. "[P]laying the fool is a delight fools cannot have" (20). "Love disposes of cats and kings, but a good stitch never parts" (54). Mathews also uses larger "pieces" of proverbs to create new proverbial combinations and permutations.

In the kingdom of the blind, few are chosen.
In the kingdom of the blind, sailors take warning:
In the kingdom of the blind, unlucky in love.
  Many are called, but the one-eyed man is king. (42)

These are declarations of dependence because the author and the texts depend on the words the culture has offered in its proverbs. In fact, *Selected Declarations of Dependence* is only a special case in the general field of writing which is always dependent on language as a given and, more particularly, on a given discourse within that language.

Along with "Their Words, For You," Mathews proposes other texts generated by combinations and permutations of proverbs. For example, the "perverb" is a hybrid, created by breaking traditional proverbs in half and joining those halves together, thus dismantling the originals and giving them new meanings. In the words of the introduction: "Every rendering was broken in half, and the halves taken with the other halves" (4). The results are often wonderful. "Red sky at night, unlucky in love." "Sticks and stones gather no moss." "Sleeping dogs spoil the broth."

Mathews creates lists of such perverbs by his own rules of combination and permutation, then offers what he calls paraphrases of his new sayings. A paraphrase is a little story that illustrates a perverb. For example: "He had won forty thousand francs at trente quarante, forty thousand dollars at chemmy, and after the casino closed, forty thousand pounds in a private poker game. Yet when I suggested he celebrate and have some champagne, he did not even answer but raised his eyes to heaven and cut the deck" (104).

The author does not tell the reader which perverb is being paraphrased by any given story. He offers four groups of paraphrase stories—106 in all—and at the end of each group he provides a list of perverbs—generated by combination and permutation—but in random order. It is up to the reader to match each paraphrase with its perverb. For instance, story 33, quoted above, is a paraphrase of the perverb "Lucky at cards, but you can't make him drink."

The perverb/paraphrase game invites the reader to play, and in fact, the play could go on indefinitely — anyone can take it up, not only by matching the perverbs and paraphrases Mathews provides but by making up new paraphrases of his or her own or even by beginning all over again with another set of proverbs which can then be broken in half, recombined according to Mathews' rules of permutation, and paraphrased. This is not simply a question of reader participation — it is an issue of the reader as a writer, although, like Mathews, the reader/writer who continues the game does so not as a privileged subject but simply as another player. Remember, Calvino insists that the combinatorial game of literature is played out "independently of the personality of the author." And in the combinatorial game that Mathews has set up, of course, the personality of the author is not and cannot be an issue.

Selected Declarations of Dependence unfolds (and continues to unfold indefinitely) beyond the modernist ideology which privileges the subject as the center of expression and self-expression as the source of authority in writing. The game Mathews initiates and the texts generated by that game — whether written by Mathews or by anyone else — are not rooted in the experiences, sensations, emotions, or thoughts of the author. Indeed, the author lacks authority here. *Selected Declarations of Dependence* is rooted in the discourse of others.

It was a "gift of words," from others —
 "from the horse's mouth"
 "from hand to mouth" (2)

But there is something else going on here, a subtle dialectical shift. If the authority of the discourse does not have its source in the author, it is also no longer rooted in the facile though often compelling cultural authority of the proverb, which Mathews' game dismantles. Here the authority is that of the text itself, as Mathews' chosen vocabulary generates meaning according to, in Calvino's words, "the possibilities intrinsic to its own material."

As we have seen, Calvino seems to argue that in a very real sense writing writes itself, and Mathews' proverb games are examples of such writing. On the other hand, Calvino also argues that sometimes the writing which writes itself can also go beyond itself to become something else.

Literature is a combinatorial game which plays on the possibilities intrinsic to its own material, independently of the personality of the author. But it is also a game which at a certain stage is invested with an unexpected meaning, a meaning having no reference at the linguistic level on which the activity takes place, but which springs from another level and brings into play something on that other level that means a great deal to the author or to the society of which he is a member. (79)

What is this "other level?" For Calvino, it is the level at which literature transcends itself, the level at which it goes beyond itself and maintains itself at the same time. Calvino writes, "The whole struggle of literature is in fact an effort to escape from the confines of language" (77). Such an escape is, of course, an impossibility; yet at that "other level" the reader recognizes that the text he reads is both equal to itself and more than itself, that the text somehow says what it says and more than it says. In such texts, literature transgresses its own boundaries in a way that still maintains those boundaries intact.

La disparition, Perec's palindrome, and *Selected Declarations of Dependence* are such texts. Mathews' text is an activity of writing within a limited discourse — the discourse of proverbs—that, by deriving its meaning from that discourse and its limitations, transcends it and extends it until it says, in a familiar form, more than it says, more than it can say, indeed what it has never said before. In a real sense, *Selected Declarations of Dependence* secures its own authority—not the authority of a subject, a writer, nor the authority of collective wisdom guaranteed by the culture at large, but the authority of "another level," the authority of a text that founds its own meaning in the process by which it writes itself into existence.

4

The Word and the Flesh: The Infinite Pornographic Text

THERE IS SOMETHING STRANGE and disturbing about the very concept of the pornographic book — from the literary classics of Sade, Apollinaire, Georges Bataille, and Pauline Réage to those garden variety, adult bookstore novels with titles like *Getting Into Each Other*, *Degraded and Delighted Waitress*, and *Club Discipline*. These are the books that have been banned, burned, and denounced on the one hand, and praised for their sexual freedom and liberating qualities on the other. On the whole, however, pornographic writing — though readily available today — remains clandestine. More often than not, it is published under pseudonyms, sold only in special stores that are set apart from the community, and bought and read by people who usually would not want to be seen doing so. Pornographic books are, in essence, written by no one for no one.

Pornography is a body of literature and a literature of the body. It is a literary genre dedicated to detailed descriptions of physical acts offered not as symbols of something else but purely for their own sake. What is strange here is not only that the limited physical possibilities of human sexuality have produced a potentially unlimited body of literature but that sex acts are the only physiological processes to have done so. Try to imagine hundreds of thousands of books written for the purpose of describing human beings sleeping or walking or sitting. Imagine detailed descriptions of the postures of sleep, the movements of walking, the positions of the seated body, descriptions that would run on for page after page. Imagine plots constructed to allow for as many such descriptions as possible in a single book, and imagine that each description is an end in itself. The sleeper does not dream, the walker is not going anywhere, the sitter sits to no purpose. The bodies are simply there, carrying out their actions in a world dedicated to sleeping, walking, sitting.

In theory at least, any bodily function could give rise to its own literary genre: blinking, salivating, eating, scratching. It is all quite absurd until one considers human sexuality. Then, quite suddenly, it is no longer necessary to imagine a body of literature devoted to such physical acts. The genre exists and thrives. It is with us, perhaps as absurd as the literature of sleeping or walking but very real.

Pornography is strange and disturbing because it is absurd. It is a writing that embodies its own unique mass of contradictions which cannot be resolved and yet which are present in every pornographic text. In fact, if such works were not self-contradictory, they could not be what they are. In a sense, erotic fiction is an impossibility that somehow has become possible.

I would also argue that erotic fiction is, in many ways, the prototypical postmodern fiction, that it provides the groundwork for much contemporary literature and literary theory from Samuel Beckett, Jorge Luis Borges, Italo Calvino, and Julio Cortázar to Michel Foucault and Jacques Derrida. The ancient category of pornography is, indeed, far more contemporary — even post-contemporary — than we might care to admit.

On the one hand, erotic fiction is fiction. Like any work of fiction, the erotic fiction is a structure of words, the product of a writer intended to be read. It would seem that erotic fiction could be analyzed and discussed in the same terms as any other fictive work. And yet, in truth, erotica is radically unlike any other type of fiction; it is essentially other.

But what is this essential otherness? To question the otherness of erotic literature is to question its very essence. It is to ask: what is it that makes the erotic work different from other literary works? Or, more positively: what are those characteristics that are present in every work of erotic fiction and that are essential for any given work to be included within this general category? What we are asking for here are those features that make a work of erotic fiction what it is and without which it might still be a work of fiction but not a work of *erotic* fiction.

It would seem that there are four essential elements common to all erotic fiction. First, there is an erotic intent. Second, there is a specific use of language typical of erotic fiction. Third, there is what might be called an erotic world view that pervades the entire genre.

And fourth, the work of erotic fiction is not simply a single text belonging to a larger body of works. Rather, all works of erotic fiction are part of a unified project — an infinite project composed over any number of generations by countless hands, an attempt to produce an infinite text that would exhaust itself completely, put an end to itself by expanding itself to infinity and transcending language by way of language. This is an impossible project, of course. The infinte text cannot be and could never be accomplished. By definition, it could not begin and could never end. It is a hopeless project, an impossibility. And yet the erotic text is such an impossible project, and it is precisely this impossibility at the heart of the pornographic project that makes erotica possible.

The Erotic Intent

There can be no question: erotic fiction is intended to arouse the (almost exclusively male) reader sexually. It is meant to have a physical effect. But while the sexual response is usually the response of one person to another, for the reader of erotic fiction it is the response of a person to a text. In general, sexual feelings join persons together, but erotica isolates the reader within himself. In the end, he is alone with the words he reads. Perhaps this is why, as Steven Marcus has pointed out: "The literature of sex, in all its branches, is not a particularly joyful or happy literature. It is on the whole rather grim and sad; even at its most intense moments there is something defeated in it."[1]

The sexual feeling inspired by another is open to fulfillment; the sexual feeling inspired by a text is not. Indeed, the only conceivable fulfillment of the erotic text would be the transformation of the text itself, the words, into sexual beings and sexual acts—into flesh. As it is, the response to erotic literature is closer to the kind of response one might have to one's own erotic thoughts. Both responses are rooted in fantasy. And yet the difference is clear, for, in responding to the

1. Steven Marcus, *The Other Victorians* (New York: Bantam, 1967), 164.

erotic text, one is reacting sexually not to one's own imagination but to the imagination of another, an imagination that has taken the form of words. In a very real sense, the erotic text is designed not only to isolate the reader but, in the end, to erase him.

The Erotic Language

Erotic literature, in its essence, is meant to arouse the reader's sexual response, and language is the vehicle of this intention, for the erotic text is nothing more than the words that make it up. Language, then, is the second element essential to erotic fiction. But the language of erotica is not language per se; it is language in the service of sexuality. It is a language sexualized so thoroughly that any word from the erotic lexicon has the power to become, in the mind of the reader, that which it represents: genitals, limbs, actions, pleasures, pains. The word becomes the arena of the erotic experience.

Works of erotic literature are literature, and works of literature are not physical objects; they are texts, assemblages of words, and they only come into existence when they are read. In the case of erotic fiction, however, the language used is specific and highly technical, as technical as the languages of physics, chemistry, or any of the other sciences. But the language of erotica, though specific to it, is not esoteric; in fact, it is known to everyone, although, like the languages of the sciences, it is the exception in everyday usage rather than the rule. Erotic language is both common and exceptional, vulgar and literary, well known and clandestine. It is a false secret, and, in a very real sense, this contradictory language, a simple combination of a very limited number of words, forms the basis of a literature of the erotic. The erotic work is and is only a specific combination of unique but ordinary words, each of which is as erotic in itself as the work taken as a whole.

Dog. Hand. Mountain. Cunt. These words are not equal by any means. For any reader of English, the word "cunt" stands out on the page; it is an obscene word, clandestine and dangerous. It is a word that is never to be used in polite society; a child who speaks it deserves to be punished. The sound of the word is rough and harsh, but, once spoken, the word itself is relatively harmless; it is gone in an instant. In print, however, "cunt" is permanent, like a scar on the page. It is more than a word; it is a thing, the thing itself, a cunt.

Dog. Hand. Mountain. Cunt. Not only does the obscene word reveal itself as unique, but it also seems to have the power to transform the words around it. Like other examples from the erotic lexicon, "cunt" establishes its own context, a context of sexuality, and it draws other words to it. The dog becomes a partner in a bestial sex act. The hand eagerly strokes the mountain of a warm breast. "Cunt" opens like a voracious mouth and engulfs the text.

The erotic language hardly seems to be a language at all. Common words, ordinary words as we use them every day, are signs that point away from themselves to what they are not. But erotic language is a system of signs that seek to become the things they signify. The impact of erotic fiction is to be found in the fact that, in the text, "prick" is not a mere sign; in a sense, it is more real than the thing it is meant to indicate. It is in this sense that Deneen Peckinpah's heroine of *Ceremonies of Love* can take in a "mouthful of cock as hard as the word."[2] The erotic word *is* its object. And, in the erotic context, other words that are usually content to remain signs also seem to take on real physical shape.

2.   Deneen Peckinpah, *Ceremonies of Love* (New York: Olympia Press, 1970), 127.

The language of erotica is an impossibility. Insofar as it is fiction, erotica is rooted in language, but insofar as it is erotic, it is a fiction that strives to become physical reality. The word is to become flesh, for only as flesh can the erotic text fulfill itself. And yet the word remains word. The eroticism of erotic literature is not an eroticism of flesh and of bodies but of print. Thus, Maurice Merleau-Ponty can write, "A good part of eroticism is on paper."[3]

This paper eroticism is difficult to understand. Erotic fiction is supposedly dangerous and often is self-consciously so, and yet the danger is only illusion, only words. The bodies are not bodies but the words for bodies; there are no sex acts, no tortures, no pains or pleasures. There are only the words: "sex," "torture," "pain," "pleasure," "danger." The pornographic project is a preordained failure. It will never be other than what it is, never be other than text. And yet there is always the hope that, if the text goes on long enough, if enough hands cover enough pages with the same magic words, the body of pornographic writing might become something it has never been and could never be. It might become real.

But there is another problem inherent to a paper eroticism. In "A note on *Story of O*," André Pieyre de Mandiargues writes: "Now, it seems fairly obvious that the time of a work of fiction, both in plot and continuity, is always a kind of past, whether or not the author likes it, whereas the time of (physical) love is specifically the present."[4] If erotica is to re-create the sex act effectively, if it is to become the sex act itself, then it must do so with immediacy, and yet the fact

3. Maurice Merleau-Ponty, *Signs*, trans. Richard C. McCleary (Evanston: Northwestern University Press, 1964), 310.
4. André Pieyre de Mandiargues, "A Note on *Story of O*," in Pauline Réage, *Story of O*, trans, Sabine d'Estrée (New York: Grove, 1967), xv–xvi.

that the sex act in this case is one of words rather than of bodies takes the entire enterprise out of the present. Print is irremediably past, and even in those erotic works which pose as "true" narratives, the writer describes scenes that supposedly have already taken place, not acts that are in fact taking place at the moment the reader experiences them.

Some writers of erotica are acutely aware of this problem. Pauline Réage begins *Story of O* in the present tense but soon gives it up, almost as if she has recognized that her attempt to make the text real and present has failed. In *Ceremonies of Love*, Peckinpah's heroine-narrator, amid vivid sexual descriptions, writes, "I suppose it would be simpler to put all this in the present tense" (13). In truth, writing erotica in the present tense is not an attempt to simplify but to make it all come true in the here and now. This is, of course, impossible, and yet the effort must be made to collapse time to a single point, indeed to transcend time, for erotic fiction is a fiction that must always strive to be somethig more than it is or ever could be.

For this reason, there is always something ironic about erotic language. For example, in *Getting Into Each Other* by E. Thomas Stearns, one finds the following: "Ted had had enough of talk. Now the time had come for him to get to know Marion in a way which would take them *beyond words*" (italics added).[5] What follows, of course, is a detailed description of a sex act that runs on for eight pages and that, needless to say, is not beyond words but is in fact nothing more than words.

Thus, erotic language hopes to escape its own nature, and yet it remains language and must. The erotic intends to be real, to be equal to what it signifies, and yet it always remains what it is — a word.

5. E. Thomas Stearns, *Getting Into Each Other* (New York: Bee Line Books, 1974), 67.

Erotic fiction cannot be what it pretends to be. It makes a promise it cannot keep. The body of the reader responds to the text, but the text is never a body; it is only and always itself. There is no communion or fulfillment, only an act of speaking that is endlessly renewed and must be, for the closure of the erotic text would be an admission of the failure that is unavoidable, though infinitely postponed. If it hopes to keep its impossible promise, *the erotic text must be infinite.*

The words that make up the erotic language are unique, but these words alone are not sufficient to explain the ways in which language functions in the erotic novel. Such words also appear in many contemporary literary works that could not be considered erotic in intent, including this one. Erotic fiction is distinguished from other texts not only by the presence of erotic words but also by the way in which the words are used. There is a very distinctive erotic style, a style that is so perfectly controlled and established that, in the case of most popular erotic fiction, it is impossible to tell the work of one author from that of another. In fact, the word "author" does not apply to the makers of textual pornography, for the words they use are not their own, nor are the rules by which they put those words together. The decision to make a work of pornography is a decision to accept the strict limits of the form and therefore to create nothing. It is the decision not to express, not even to write in the accepted sense of that term, but to repeat. The maker of the pornographic text is not author but scribe, medieval copyist — an anachronism. There are advantages in pursuing this obsolete calling, as Italo Calvino has shown: "The copyist lived simultaneously in two temporal dimensions, that of reading and that of writing; he could write without the anguish of having the void open before his pen; read without the anguish of having his own act become concrete in some material object." [6]

Like the scribe, pornographers are not called upon to invent, to have "something to say." That is not their job. Rather, they do again what has already been done, re-create that which already is, not as an artist might draw an image to represent some object in the real world but as someone might use onionskin paper to trace an already completed drawing of a fantastic creature or landscape that could not possibly exist. The act of tracing, of writing again, is a manner of reading, but this is an act of reading that reads only what it writes and writes only what it reads.

And yet, though they have much in common with the medieval copyist, pornographers are not as anachronistic as they might seem. In our time, philosophy and literary theory have begun to call the traditional concept of the author into question, and this questioning of the authority of the author goes beyond the tight restrictions of pornography and literary genres to address the whole of writing, the generation of texts.

Language and the rules by which language takes shape as novels, plays, poems, works of history, philosophy, physics, or biology, letters, diaries, newspapers, and catalogues — these make writing possible, and thus they make authorship possible as well. But there is a sense in which any author's text is already implicit in this language and these rules of composition. What we call writing would seem to be the realization of a potential text, the discovery of a text hidden more or less well in the possibilities of language, possibilities and language that the author did not create. Writing then is accomplished not through personal expression but through those

6. Italo Calvino, *If on a winter's night a traveler,* trans. William Weaver (New York: Harcourt Brace Jovanovich, 1981), 178.

very barriers to personal expression—the language of others and the rules of textuality—that make writing possible. "As a result," according to Michel Foucault, "the mark of the writer is reduced to nothing more than the singularity of his absence; he must assume the role of the dead man in the game of writing."[7]

The language the writer writes compromises the author, who must absent himself or herself as subject if he or she is to engage in writing. Writing, even before it begins, has already created an arena for performance in which the author's performance is the erasure of self. Writing is "a question of creating a space into which the writing subject constantly disappears" (142).

Thus, the person of the author, his self, and his capacity for expression are clearly open to question. Writers and critics in our time have come to this knowledge slowly and without enthusiasm. Pornographers have always known. The pornographic text has always erased its authors in favor of itself. Other literary genres—history, biography, etc.—also try to suppress creativity and personal authority in order to maintain themselves, but pornography is *in its essence* an authorless text. The style, language, and structure of pornography are impersonal, detached, and, in theory at least, eternal. It is because of this impersonal style that the pornographic text can and must be continued and passed on from writer to writer, through an infinite chain of writers, each of whom disappears at the moment he or she begins to write.

The pornographic text is rooted in urgency as infinite repetition; the words are presented as incantations, as mystical formulas. The repetition of a limited number of secret words

7. Michel Foucault, "What Is an Author?" in Josué V. Harari, ed., *Textual Strategies* (Ithaca: Cornell University Press, 1979), 142-43.

in various combinations is important, for only in infinite repetition can the words have any hope of magically becoming the bodies and acts they represent. Of course, the magical incantations can never complete the transformation, but the intent is there. Like prayers or religious rituals, erotic language is meant to make present that which is eternally absent, to re-create in real time and space that which exists in its own abstract, transcendent realm, or that which does not exist at all. This religious aspect of erotica is essential to the genre, though what is being summoned by the incantations is not a god or a spirit; it is flesh in sexual contact. The transformation, always promised but never fulfilled, would be of a text into a reality that no longer needs erotic language in order to exist. The perfect erotic language, then, would be one which put an end to itself, exhausted itself by speaking itself to infinity.

The Erotic World View

Erotic literature, in its essence, is meant to arouse the reader's sexual response, and language is the vehicle of this intention. But there is a third characteristic that encompasses the entire project of erotica. In a real sense, the intention to arouse sexual responses and the erotic use of language, though essential to erotic literature, are only means to an end, and that end is the complete sexualization of the world beyond the page. In theory, the erotic text would become the whole of reality.

Clearly, a project that seeks to transform all of reality is an extreme one, and yet erotic literature is such a project. By its own nature, the erotic text seeks to go beyond itself, to become real; this in itself is an impossibility, but even if it were possible for words to magically become flesh, it would still not be enough. For the erotic text to truly complete itself, it would have to become not merely real but the whole of reality, the only reality. It would have to transform the universe into an infinite sexual cosmos. And that transformation of our world by the pornographic text could only be accomplished by defining the being of our world according to a pornographic onto-theology—by transforming the language we use to speak and to proclaim our reality into a pornographic language that speaks only the possibilities of flesh.

In erotic literature, sex is the ordering principle of the universe, the substructure of Being itself. In this universe, all men and all women are totally sexual beings; they live only for sexual contact, both as subjects and as objects. And every object in this universe can be enlisted for sexual use or granted sexual powers.

This is the metaphysical aspect of erotic fiction, and it is a metaphysics which, though primitive, is still surprisingly sophisticated. Like all philosophical universes, the erotic universe is carefully structured and ordered; it is what the word "universe" implies—a whole, a unity.

The erotic metaphysics presents a structural whole based upon a sexuality that pervades all of Being. What is exists only insofar as it is sexualized; sex, then, is the cause and purpose not only of all life but of all that is or ever could be.

In the erotic universe, all beings are charged with a sexual significance. It is true that all objects and settings can be put to sexual use and gain their very existence and meaning from such use, but the sexualization of the world goes beyond such practical aspects. In *Story of O*, the chains, whips, and instruments of torture and bondage are used for sexual purposes, but even when they are not in use on O's body, they lie in wait as images of the principles which structure O's world.

A more subtle, more profound example of the sexualized object is found in Jean de Berg's *The Image*:

Anne held her right hand out toward the half-opened flower. Very gently she ran her finger tips around the outer edges of the petals, partly closed, barely touching their slender pink flesh. She ran her fingers several times around the closed heart, very slowly. Then she delicately spread open the inner petals and closed them again, using all five fingers.

When she had, in this fashion, spread wide and closed again the flower's center two or three times, she suddenly thrust her middle finger deep inside it, where it almost disappeared entirely. Then she withdrew her finger, very slowly, only to plunge it in again as far as it would go.[8]

It is a game of words. By describing the rose in the same terms he would use to describe a woman's genitals, de Berg transforms the flowers that appear throughout the book into vehicles of sexuality and, in time, of torture and domination. Or, again: "Between her legs parted by the gas tank, the motor throbs with all the power of its two enormous cylinders, a living thing, trembling and so furious that such frenzy amazes her as much as at the first moment it was revealed to her. What a brute!"[9] The quotation is from de Mandiargues' novel *The Motorcycle*, and here the title "character" becomes a male member because the machine and the human organ are described in the same terms. It is a game of words, but a dangerous one, for the words that become sexualized through the erotic text are also the words of our world. To read such texts, then, is to risk the chastity of our own language.

8. Jean de Berg, *The Image*, trans. Patsy Southgate (New York: Grove, 1967), 32.
9. André Pieyre de Mandiargues, *The Motorcycle*, trans. Richard Howard (New York: Grove, 1965), 25.

Although human sexuality forms the core of erotic literature, the erotic universe is not a human universe. Man is not at the center of this world; he is only a vehicle for the expression of the sexual force that structured Being before he came into existence and that will control the universe after he is gone. Thus, the characters in erotic fiction are rarely characters as they are found in other literary works. In erotica, characters are sexualized into nonpersons; they are sexual forces or sexual objects or both.

This is why the erotic character is not psychological but physiological. He is equal to his body; in the last analysis, he is nothing more than his physical description.

Like the characters, the settings in erotic fiction are also sexualized through this game of words. It is not only that every possible place is a potential sexual arena, though this is certainly the case. Like characters, settings are no more than their physical descriptions, and those descriptions subject rooms, landscapes, mountaintops, whatever, to the principle of sexuality.

Erotic fiction is set in sexualized space, space that is closed and isolated. More often than not, the setting is not outdoors but indoors, not natural but man-made; it is luxurious, with sumptuous beds, velvet pillows, silk sheets. Even the dungeons and torture chambers bear the signs of privilege; the chains and whips are custommade and monogrammed, and all instruments are crafted to suit the preferences of the sexual masters.

Erotic space is tightly closed and self-contained, set apart and detached from the rest of the world. It is a world unto itself. In fact, it is *the* world. Nothing exists beyond Sade's Chateau de Silling or Réage's Roissy; the walls of these womblike structures are the walls of the universe, and within all is ordered and controlled by the metaphysical sex principle. There are no seams or cracks, no flaws; erotic space is perfectly contained. It is a universe in which every being has a purpose, and, though dangerous and deadly to the body, it is a place of safety for the mind, because it is a universe that is capable of complete and perfect explanation.

Erotic space, contained as it is, is still spatial, but time in erotic fiction can hardly be called time at all. We have seen that erotica must deal with the problem of transcending the past time of the printed word in order to transform that past into the eternal present of sexuality. The erotic work attempts to do this by denying time as we in the West understand it.

In the West, time is linear, leading from past to present to future; the world and people within the world are historical, and the historical is subject to change, growth, progression, and dissolution. Western religion is eschatological, based on a belief in the eventual closure of time in favor of eternity, and, for the most part, this eschatological view of time has been taken over by Western philosophy and science.

But the sexualized time of erotic literature is neither linear nor eschatological, and it is not the traditional chronological time of conventional fiction with its Aristotelian beginning, middle, and end. The time of erotic literature is circular, repetitious, ahistorical, because the plot that generates time in nonerotic fiction is only a minimal characteristic of erotica. In erotic fiction, plot is little more than an excuse for the presentation of sexual scenes that are all basically alike. Thus "before" and "after" in erotic time mean simply earlier or later in the text; there is no temporal flow, and there is rarely a profound sense of change or progress in erotic fiction. Nor is there ever a sense of closure, for almost every erotic novel ends with a sexual encounter, thus folding the text back upon itself. Erotic time is circular and infinite, endless and therefore timeless.

On the surface, it might seem absurd to discuss erotica in such profoundly metaphysical terms, and yet there can be no doubt that there is an erotic metaphysics and an erotic theology. Metaphysically, the erotic universe is structured upon the sex principle; this is basic. But the erotic theology, the religion of erotica, is founded upon a dialectical movement that is more difficult to chart.

Sacrilege is a commonplace in erotica; the literature is full of libertine priests, monks, and nuns, sex acts that profane churches, altars, and the Host, and equivalents of the ancient black sabbaths of witchcraft. However, erotic literature must secretly champion religion in order for its sacrilege to be effective. Passages in erotica may be blasphemous, but blasphemy is only effective if the speaker truly believes that there is a God to insult; for a nonbeliever, sacrilege is an impossibility. Therefore, no matter how profane erotic literature seems to be, it is never atheistic. God and the Church are essential to erotica. In a sense, erotic fiction, in its sacrilege, offers an interesting argument for the existence of God: God must exist because He can be offended.

Like witchcraft, erotica needs God, and, also like witchcraft, erotic fiction proposes an antireligion which is actually the old religion in disguise. Erotic literature has its martyrs, and the descriptions of erotic martyrdom are not so very different from accounts of the lives of the saints. Thus, in *Story of O*, Pauline Réage writes: "Beneath the gazes, beneath the hands, beneath the sexes that defiled her, the whips that rent her, she lost herself in a delirious absence from herself which returned her to love, and, perhaps, brought her to the edge of death" (39). Or, again, in the sequel, *Return to the Chateau*: "A terrible, grotesque image crossed her mind: the calvary of St. George. Yes, perhaps she was the lowest representation of that same calvary, on her knees and supported by her elbows, straddled by unknown men."[10]

In these passages, O becomes a saint of the erotic, but her god is not the God of the Judaeo-Christian religions; it is the pantheistic deity of sex, the ordering principle of the erotic universe, and its icons are the implements of sex, particularly the parts of the body which carry out the sexual functions. The following, with its erotic-religious reference, is chosen almost at random and is not uncommon in the literature. "He ran his fingers through her raven-black hair now as she brought his erection to its full glory. It stood tall and large and he loved the way she adored it; in fact, seemed to be worshipping at the thing as though it were some kind of god."[11]

In erotica, cocks are gods, bodies are altars, semen is the Host. The masters of sexuality are the priests of the new religion, their victims are its martyrs, and the sex act itself is the holy ritual, repeated again and again in strict accord with holy canon amid a litany of obscenities. The religious pretensions of erotica are profound, and this should not be surprising, for, as David Pirie has pointed out, there seems to be something about our views of sex as a source of fantasy that links sexuality and the supernatural in the human mind.[12] As a result, the sacrilege of erotic fiction is not only an attempt to maintain the traditional Christian theology intact; it is also

10.   Pauline Réage, *Return to the Chateau*, trans., Sabine d'Estree (New York: Grove, 1973), 29–30.

11.   Andrea Herty, *Chained to Desire* (New York: Bee Line Books, 1978), 52.

12.   David Pirie, *The Vampire Cinema* (New York: Crescent Books, 1977), 98.

an attempt to establish a new theology designed to coexist with the old — a new theology which, rather than serving as protest against traditional orthodoxy, is perhaps more strict and more conservative than the religion it pretends to rival.

There is also an erotic moral philosophy that is linked to the erotic theology and that has its roots in the governing principle of sexuality in the eroticized universe. In general, the sex acts found in erotic literature are represented as free and natural, as good, regardless of how bizarre or deadly they might be. This stands to reason: if the principle of sexuality governs the universe, then acts which are in accord with that principle must be good, for the participants in such acts are acting out what could be termed their divine purpose; they are acting in the service of the erotic godhead.

Because sexuality is presented as free and good, it is common to hear erotica defended on the basis of the sexual freedom it seems to espouse. However, there is nothing free about erotic fiction, for its very existence and effectiveness are linked to the traditional Christian view of sexuality as evil. If sexuality were no longer considered evil, if the sexual functions of the body were suddenly no more dangerous than other physical functions like sleeping, eating, or walking, there would no longer be a need for an entire body of literature dedicated to the physiology of the erotic. Thus, erotic fiction must embrace the traditional concepts of Good and Evil it appears to attack, just as it must embrace the Church and the Deity it seems to reject, and it must relegate itself to the world of Evil; it must argue for sexual freedom, but the argument cannot be a perfect one. If it were, erotica would simply cease to exist; the erotic text would consume itself in its own logic.

There can be no question: erotic fiction is intended to arouse the reader sexually. And this is also true — it is intented to arouse the reader by means that are clandestine, guilt-ridden, evil. This is not to say that erotica *is* evil or ever could be. Erotic literature does not intend to do evil, to create evil, or to espouse evil. Rather, it is meant to *appear* to be evil; it accepts and even welcomes the definition civilization has offered it. Individual works of erotic fiction rarely if ever *seem* to be aware of themselves as openly evil; in fact, sexuality in erotic literature is depicted as natural and guilt-free. And yet each work presents the illusion of evil. If it did not, and if society refused to acknowledge the evil of literary sexuality, erotica would simply cease to be.

Despite these dialectical movements, however, the erotic world view is basically a coherent one. Space, time, persons, and objects are subjugated to the principle of sexuality. It is for this reason that Steven Marcus has referred to the world of erotic literature as a utopian fantasy, a "pornotopia" (271).

For Marcus, pornotopia is the realm where all that is nonsexual is either excluded or sexualized, and all of erotic fiction is set within this world. His analysis of the pornotopia is intelligent and thoughtful but not quite accurate. Marcus is saying that a pornotopia is a place (or, more strictly, a nonplace) where sexuality is imposed upon the natural world, either by putting nonsexual objects to sexual use or by excluding them completely. In a sense, he is correct, but the erotic philosophy is not intended to be one that is imposed on a preexisting world in a way that, for example, a political philosophy is imposed upon or takes shape within a world where that philosophy did not exist before. Rather, the erotic philosophy is a metaphysical philosophy, a religious philosophy; that is, it outlines not the way things ought to be in a perfect world (which the term "utopia" — and therefore "pornotopia" — implies) but the way things *are* in fact. The erotic world view intends to chart the very nature of the universe. It states that all of Being is ordered according to the principle of sexuality and that this principle preexists any given aspect of creation, much as the Christian God preexists the world He governs. The erotic philosophy is not, therefore, pornotopian but *cosmoerotic*.

If the pure work of erotica were possible, if there could be a novel that totally fulfilled the intent to sexually arouse the reader on every page and with every word, that completely eroticized its language and sexualized the universe, it would be something of a revolutionary masterpiece, because, as Tzvetan Todorov has pointed out, "the masterpiece of popular literature is precisely the book which best fits its genre."[13] Such a work would change not only the world of literature but the real world as well. Language would no longer be suited for any purpose other than sexuality, and the cosmoerotic principle would be the principle of the real universe beyond the text.

And yet such a work, in all its perfection, would also be totally predictable, repetitious, and dull. In fact, it would not be a literary work at all, though it is difficult to know what it would be. Clearly, it would be "the book which best fits its genre," but, as Todorov also notes, "the best [genre] novel will be the one about which there is nothing to say" (43).

The Infinite Erotic Text

Of course, there can never be a perfect work of erotic fiction in this sense, and the project of erotic writing does not aim toward the realization of that single, singular text. Instead,

13. Tzvetan Todorov, *The Poetics of Prose*, trans. Richard Howard (Ithaca: Cornell University Press, 1977), 43.

the project of erotic writing is the production of an infinite text — without beginning or end, composed by infinite hands rewriting the same words again and again and again.

But why does the erotic text project itself to infinity? The erotic work hopes to say all that has ever been said, all that ever could be said, perhaps even that which never could be said — a truth beyond speaking. The erotic text, extended to infinity, would speak the unspeakable. Indeed, the infinite erotic text would exhaust its own language completely and perhaps reach that secret silence beyond language where speaking equals doing, where word equals flesh.

Erotic prose is not intended to represent; it is intended to *be,* to create a real world that could exist apart from the page, a page that would in fact disappear in favor of that reality. This is impossible, of course; the infinite erotic text is an impossibility. It could never be accomplished and so could never go beyond itself to become reality. It is for this reason that there is a sense of frustration and (though the term seems inappropriate) impotence in all erotic prose. The text, no matter how detailed, extended, or graphic, is never enough.

The infinite erotic text is an impossibility. But if it were possible, even in theory, what might it be? Like infinite space or infinite time, it would be that which can be named and perhaps conceived but never accomplished. The history of human writing has not produced an infinite text and never will. And yet the idea of an infinite text has meaning. Such a text would be unwritable, unreadable, but it can be imagined, dreamed of, pursued.

The very idea of an infinite text, like the idea of pornography itself, is strange and disturbing, even frightening, for if such a thing were possible, it would speak beyond the individual speaker/writer/reader, beyond the history of all speakers and writers and readers. This text would speak all truths — the secret meaning of things, perhaps secrets no one would ever want to be spoken. The same text would also speak all lies, all contradictions, all gibberish, all madness. It would oppose itself at every turn, cancel itself out, erase itself. It would be both infinte speech and infinite silence.

The Divine Marquis

The perfect example of the infinite erotic project as the attempt to "speak everything," to achieve an actual infinity that might transform the speech of words into the silence of flesh, is found in the works of the writer who established the language and the form of pornography — the Marquis de Sade. Sade was, of course, the quintessential speaker of the unspeakable whose cultural revolution is still in progress. Late in the eighteenth century, Sade wrote a series of voluminous works, including *Justine, Juliette,* and *The 120 Days of Sodom*, works that have been banned universally as disruptive, corrupting, negative, infinitely evil. Only recently have these fictions become available once more, and though they have been discussed often by literary critics, psychologists, and philosophers in the past few years, Western civilization is still a long way from assimilating these works by the master of rational, systematic cruelty.

For Sade, writing is always revolutionary, disruptive, "the perpetual immoral subversion of the existing order."[14] With their seemingly infinite descriptions of rapes, beatings, and sexual murders, with their lengthy excursions into a philosophy of evil, Sade's writings seek to go beyond the limits of the language that makes them possible. Sade proceeds toward

14. Angela Carter, *The Sadean Woman and the Ideology of Pornography* (New York: Harper and Row, 1980), 91.

those limits by way of logic, order, and infinite repetition, as if the hundreds and millions of words he writes might in time collapse under their own weight, like a dead star that leaves a black hole in its wake. The goal here is a passing over, a going beyond, a transforming of the reality of language into a reality that is not only words. It is in this sense that Maurice Blanchot has written, "We can safely state, without fear of unduly modernizing Sade's thought, that he was one of the first thinkers of his century to have recognized and incorporated into his world view the notion of transcendence."[15]

Sade's goal, then, was the transcendence of language by way of language, the total collapse of the difference between word and thing, or, in the words of Georges Bataille:

[Sade] had as his goal the clear consciousness of suppression—of the difference between subject and object. Thus his goal only differed from that of philosophy by the path he chose in order to attain it: Sade started with an examination of violent "releases" in practice which he wanted to make intelligibile while philosophy starts from a calm consciousness—from distinct intelligibility—in order to bring it to a point of fusion.[16]

Of course, Sade's project involves the infinite project of pornography in a hopeless contradiction. The language that transcends itself gives way to a new language; the speaking of the unspeakable is a new kind of speaking. In discussing Sade's work, Roland Barthes has maintained that the marquis is the founder of a new language, created "precisely in order to say nothing, to observe a vacancy."[17] Sade's is an erotic

15. Maurice Blanchot, "Sade," in *The Marquis de Sade: "Justine," "Philosophy in the Bedroom" and Other Writings,* trans. Richard Seaver and Austryn Wainhouse (New York: Grove, 1965), 63.

16. Georges Bataille, *Literature and Evil,* trans. Alastair Hamilton (London: Calder and Boyars, 1973), 93-94.

17. Roland Barthes, *Sade/Fourier/Loyola,* trans. Richard Miller (New York: Hill and Wang, 1976), 156-57.

language, of course, the language that has made the history of pornography possible. According to Barthes, it is language, Sadean language, that turns simple acts into pornography, into crime, into evil.

Let us (if we can) imagine a society without language. Here is a man copulating with a woman, *a tergo*, and using in the act a bit of wheat paste. On this level, no perversion. Only by the progressive addition of some nouns does the crime gradually *develop*, grow in volume, in consistency, and attain the highest degree of transgression. The man is called the *father* of the woman he is possessing, who is described as being *married*; the amorous act is ignominiously termed *sodomy*; and the bit of bread bizarrely associated in this act becomes, under the noun *host*, a religious symbol whose flouting is sacrilege. Sade excells in *collecting* this pile of language: for him, the sentence has this function of founding crime: the syntax, refined by centuries of culture, becomes an *elegant* . . . art; it collects crime with exactitude and address: "To unite incest, adultery, sodomy, and sacrilege, he buggers his married daughter with a host." (156 — 57)

Here is an example of the paradox of pornographic writing. Sade writes in order to transcend the written, to reach from the text into reality, to transform the said into the done. And he succeeds in saying that which, in his time and in ours, could not and cannot be said. But, paradoxically, in speaking beyond the speakable, he transcends speech not into a reality beyond words but into a reality that is *only* words, new words, Sadean words. As Barthes shows, Sade's crimes are rooted in language, are crimes only because there are words that make them so. Sade speaks a tale that passes over into the Sadean criminal myth to transcend the storiness of the story, and yet, paradoxically, the escape *from* language is an escape *to* a new language that points not into the world beyond words but back to itself.

For Sade, writing is a criminal act, certainly an act that could potentially revolutionize the culture in which it comes to light. But what does Sade or any writer hope to gain from committing such acts? In his analysis of Sade's work, Pierre Klossowski recalls the biblical myth of the first crime, the eating of the fruit from the Tree of Knowledge, committed by Adam, the first speaker, the creator of language. Klossowski says: "If [in the Garden of Eden] knowledge ends by becoming a crime, what we call crime must contain the key to knowledge. As a result, it is only by extending the sphere of crime further and further that mind, reaching those *extraordinary crimes*, will recover its lost knowledge—that knowledge which is infinitely greater than what we have."[18]

The goal of the infinite erotic text, then, would be to establish "the realm in which opposites are destroyed and conjoined. Only these abysses, these conjunctions, can give us the truth" (Bataille, 155).

But this is a knowledge—a truth—beyond words, a knowledge that even writing which transcends itself cannot reach, perhaps because it does not exist. If writing is a criminal act, it is so not because it discovers knowledge but because it creates it . . . *in words*. This is Sade's goal. His new language is the language of textual eroticism, but it is also the language of modern literature—of Joyce, Beckett, Borges, and the postmodernists who have come after. It is the language that goes beyond itself and its knowledge by reflecting on itself and its own mode of knowing, by limiting itself to speaking speech, by betraying itself as only words and yet something more which, in its turn, is also only words.

18. Pierre Klossowski, "Nature as Destructive Principle," in *The Marquis de Sade: The 120 Days of Sodom and Other Writings*, trans. Richard Seaver and Austryn Wainhouse (New York: Grove, 1966), 74. Hereafter cited as *120 Days*.

Sade's literary language is the perfect illustration of literature as a combinatorial game, and his playing pieces are the various possibilities of sexual crime, shuffled and reshuffled indefinitely with an interchangeable cast of characters to generate the Sadean scene.

> In the scene, all functions can be interchanged, everyone can and must be in turn agent and patient, whipper and whipped, coprophagist and coprophagee, etc. This is a cardinal rule, first because it assimilates Sadian eroticism into a truly formal language, where there are only classes of actions, not groups of individuals, which enormously simplifies its grammar: the subject of the action (in the grammatical sense) can just as readily be a libertine, an assistant, a victim, a wife. . . . (Barthes, 30)

This is precisely the game, invented by Sade, that every pornographer plays. It is the game of that genre, (re)-created by authors who consent to play by those rules. Thus, as we have seen, pornographic works are identical, authorless. It is for this reason that Susan Sontag could write: "Experiences aren't pornographic; only images and representations — structures of the imagination — are. That is why a pornographic book often can make the reader think of, mainly, other pornographic books."[19]

Still, Sade's writings are exceptional, not only because he invented the rules of the game but because he tried to exhaust all of its possibilities single-handedly. The game consists of a number of characters (or caricatures) and a number of sexual acts, and, to Sade, playing that game honestly meant offering not merely a few combinations of acts and characters but every possible permutation of the elements, played out with mathematical precision. The unfinished *120 Days of Sodom* is the book that was supposed to exhaust those per-

19. Susan Sontag, *Styles of Radical Will* (New York: Delta, 1978), 49.

mutations, to be both within the genre of pornography and at the same time the whole of the genre.

It was an impossible dream that Sade abandoned in a cell in the Bastille, though not by choice. The work was lost, apparently forever, and it was not found again until early in the twentieth century. Not surprisingly, Sade was crushed, for he had to leave the ultimate game unfinished. The noted scholar of the marquis' life and works, Maurice Heine, explains just how important the work was to its author: "Losing his *120 Days*, Sade lost his main thread and knew it. The remainder of his literary life was dominated by concern to remedy the consequences of that accident. So with painful perserverance and insistence he went on striving to attain the mastery which was his when at the height of his solitude and misanthropy."[20]

It seems unlikely that Sade could ever have finished this work. Even in its present form, *The 120 Days of Sodom* runs to hundreds of thousands of words, including more than a hundred pages of notes for scenes yet to be written. The number of permutations of characters and acts within the work would have approached infinity, and Sade was concerned that, in his impossible attempt to exhaust them, even he might become confused. In a note to himself at the end of part 2, he writes: "When I later put the text in final order, I must be particularly careful to have a notebook beside me at all times; I'll have to put down very exact mention of each happening and each portrait as I write it; otherwise, I'll get horribly confused because of the multitude of characters" (*120 Days*, 570).

The book that was intended to be both the particular and the universal of its genre was never completed, and yet, even incomplete as it is, it is an infinite text, for it established the

20. Quoted in Gilbert Lély, *The Marquis de Sade,* trans. Alec Brown (New York: Grove, 1970), 306.

rules for a game that can never be played out to its end—the game of pornographic literature.

Sade is the classic teller of erotic tales, a master of infinite repetition and variation. He knows that the goal of writing is the transcendence not only of the old language and the old culture but also of the writer. This is a familiar paradox and, perhaps, an unspeakable truth that is spoken here; the writer is present in the writing through the traces he or she has left, and yet the writing can only go beyond itself to become "reality" when the writer is effaced. Sade finds the possibility for his own annihilation by going to the extremes of rigor, logic, and precision, by generating a form of fiction that all but writes itself and could do so to infinity. He is totally committed to his thought, and, as Maurice Blanchot has pointed out, "The internal man, who asserts himself completely, is also completely destroyed" (66).

Sade wanted nothing more than to erase himself. In his last testament, he wrote out instructions for his funeral: "Once the grave is filled in, acorns are to be scattered over it, so that in time the grave is again overgrown, and when the undergrowth is grown as it was before, the traces of my grave will vanish from the face of the earth as I like to think memory of me will be effaced from men's minds" (Lely 461).

Sade's infinite project was precisely this effort to efface himself. The infinite text and the writing of the infinite text—the product that is infinitely deferred and the process by which the completed product is both brought into being and infinitely postponed—survive beyond the person whose name appears on the opening page. The infinite text exhausts the very idea of "the writer," for it is the text itself that holds authority over the author. Again, according to Georges Bataille, "the true sense of an infinitely profound work is to be found in the author's desire to disappear, to vanish without leaving a human trace, because nothing else is worthy of him" (89).

But there is something else at work here, another erasure, perhaps another unspeakable truth. Sade creates representations of extreme cruelty, but his books are acts of cruelty in their own right, directed against the reader. His fictions offend every sensibility, every moral tenet, every article of faith; no reader could read Sade and agree with him, and so every reader is violated by these texts. But, as Blanchot notes, "Cruelty is nothing more than the negation of self" (68), in this case the self of Sade and the self of the reader.

The erasure of the reader is the consequence of any act of writing, for the reader is the reader only insofar as he or she reads, and yet the act of reading that consumes the text also consumes the reader *as reader*. The reader erases himself, and this process is complete when he turns the last page of the book.

But if the reader is erased by every text he reads as he reads it, the infinite erotic text would not only erase him but exhaust and transform him, as it would exhaust and transform every aspect of the real.

In erasing the writer and the reader, in its effort to extend itself to infinity, to transcend itself, to become both more and less than itself, the erotic text is the prototype for the infinite circle of *Finnegans Wake*, the infinite chain of voices in Samuel Beckett's trilogy, the infinite combinations and permutations of Julio Cortázar's *Hopscotch*, the infinite game of Italo Calvino's *The Castle of Crossed Destinies*, and many other postmodern works that generate themselves and project themselves into the infinite future in hopes of transcending their own language in favor of that unspeakable silence that might lie just beyond the realm of the speakable.

And what is this secret silence, this unspeakable secret that the infinite text might yet speak? There is no way of knowing, of course. The truly unspeakable is not to be spoken, just as the truly infinite text is not to be accomplished. And yet, if, as Italo Calvino suggests, "the whole struggle of literature is in fact an effort to escape from the confines of language"[21] — which is clearly the aim of the erotic project — and if the potentially infinite text is an effort to make good that escape, the author of such a text must have some sense of what he or she hopes to achieve.

Perhaps the pornographer wants only what every person wants and has always wanted. The infinite text allows the author to transcend himself or herself, to speak beyond time, life, death. It is immortality, of a sort. The infinite text speaks the unspeakable, for it speaks into the unknown, into a future neither writer nor reader will ever see. It is, then, a sacred text, replacing God and personal immortality with a speech that goes beyond the personal, beyond the self. Death is the silence beyond speaking, but if there can be a speaking even beyond that silence, then there is no death, only the selfless voice that eternally speaks itself into being.

The erotic text, as an infinite project, projects one possible answer — an impossible answer — to an impossible question of infinite importance.

The death of God is . . coeval with access to the impossible, since God marks the outer limit of thought and experience . . . , the rational limit beyond which meaning and experience dissolve into nothingness. The deity is the object of mystical experience, but also the fountainhead of reason, the father, and the source of the word. The deity is the origin of an order in which all things remain subordinate to the possible. But once it is dead, what will fill the void?[22]

21.   Italo Calvino, "Myth in the Narrative," trans. Erica Freiberg, in Raymond Federman, ed., *Surfiction: Fiction Now and Tomorrow* (Chicago: Swallow press, 1975), 77.
22.   Michele H. Richman, *Reading Georges Bataille: Beyond the Gift* (Baltimore: Johns Hopkins University Press, 1982), 71.

Part 3

The Authority of the Reader

5

The Reader Who Reads and the Reader Who is Read: A Reading of Italo Calvino's *If on a winter's night a traveler*

1

You are about to begin reading Italo Calvino's new novel, *If on a winter's night a traveler.*

WITH THIS SIMPLE SENTENCE, Italo Calvino opens not only a new novel (the novel the reader has also opened) but the entire realm of writing, reading, the written, and the read. In fact, there is nothing simple here. The reader of this sentence becomes, through the act of reading it, a character in the fiction (the you, the read). Quite unexpectedly, he or she is doubled and erased. Sitting in a living room, in a library, on a park bench, on a bus, the reader is suddenly introduced as the main character of a novel he or she has not yet read.

This reader in the real world beyond the fiction finds that he has been fictionalized, that he must read himself into existence, constitute himself in the act of reading.

Who is this reader who reads himself? He is the Reader who reads and the Reader who is read. He is the source of *If on a winter's night a traveler*, first as the protagonist whose acts make the novel happen and again as the one whose acts (of reading) transform the novel from a printed text into a personal experience. Without a reader, there could be no novel, and yet it is the novel that makes the reader what he or she is.

Who is this Reader? And what is this novel that introduces itself by name in the opening sentence but never seems to appear? What (who) is it that the Reader reads?

2

The traps are one inside the other, and they all snap shut at the same time.

Italo Calvino's remarkable novel *If on a winter's night a traveler* is such a multiple trap for the reader, though it is a trap that is closed in upon itself and yet open at every point. It is a fiction about fiction, a writing about writing, a to-be-read about reading. It is also the story of the Reader's search for the novel he wants to read, in this case Italo Calvino's *If on a winter's night a traveler*, a novel which quite possibly does not exist. It is a story which contains many stories, including its own. Silas Flannery, one of the many (fictional) authors of subfictions within the main fiction of *If on a winter's night a travel* keeps a (fictional) diary in which he takes (fictional) notes for a (fictional) (still-to-be-written) novel.

I have had the idea of writing a novel composed only of beginnings of novels. The protagonist could be a Reader who is continually interrupted. The Reader buys the new novel A by the author Z. But it is a defective copy, he can't go beyond the beginning. . . . He returns to the bookshop to have the volume exchanged. . . .

I could write it all in the second person: you, Reader. . . . I could also introduce a young lady, the Other Reader, and a counterfeit translator, and an old writer who keeps a diary like this diary. . . .[1]

This is the story of *If on a winter's night a traveler*, told within that story by one of its own characters. But this is not the story of the *If on a winter's night a traveler* the Reader wants to read. He (you) begins to read *If on a winter's night a traveler*, the story of a secret agent stranded in a provincial railway station during a dangerous mission, but he soon finds that his copy of the book does not contain the whole tale; in fact, because of an error in binding, his volume only repeats the beginning of the story again and again. He returns to the bookstore to get another copy of *If on a winter's night a traveler*, only to learn that the story he wants is actually *Outside the town of Malbork*, a Polish novel by Tazio Bazakbal which was accidentally bound in the covers of *If on a winter's night a traveler*. Unfortunately, when he begins to read Bazakbal's book, he realizes that this is not the novel he started reading earlier.

In his search for the story he wants, he learns that what he thought was a novel by Tazio Bazakbal is actually (not) Ukko Ahti's *Leaning from the steep slope* which is (not) *Without fear of wind or vertigo* by Vorts Viljandi which is (not) Bertrand Vandervelde's *Looks down in the gathering shadow* which is (not) Silas Flannery's *In a network of lines*

---

1. Italo Calvino, *If on a winter's night a traveler*, trans. William Weaver (New York: Harcourt Brace Jovanovich, 1981), 197–98.

that enlace which is (not) (quite) *In a network of lines that intersect* which is (not) *On the carpet of leaves illuminated by the moon* by Takakumi Ikoka which is (not) Calixto Bandera's *Around an empty grave* which is (not) Anatoly Anatolin's *What story down there awaits its end?* None of these novels continues the story which was (perhaps) (perhaps not) *If on a winter's night a traveler* by Italo Calvino; the Reader reads the opening chapter of each fiction, but, in each case, he never gets beyond the beginning. Between readings, he becomes involved with the Other Reader (Ludmilla), her sister Lotaria, and Ermes Marana, the outlaw translator who heads the Organization of Apocryphal Power, a literary terrorist group. Soon the Reader is involved in international intrigue that is far more mysterious and exciting than any of the novels he has not quite read.

In fact, the novels by Ahti, Vandervelde, Flannery, Anatolin, et al. are plagiarisms, translations, and mistranslations of each other; like *If on a winter's night a traveler,* they are fictional fictions, beginnings without endings, texts generated by and pointing to other texts.

What then is *If on a winter's night a traveler?* It is the whole and the part, the container and the contained, the text which encompasses the subtexts and which makes them possible.

3

This book so far has been careful to leave open to the Reader who is reading the possibility of identifying himself with the Reader who is Read.

And who is the Reader in/of *If on a winter's night a traveler?* Within the text, he is the Reader in search of the novel which brings him into existence, the novel in which he is a character. But he is also the Reader of the opening chapters of *If on a winter's night a traveler* and nine other fictions within the fiction. He is a Reader in *If on a winter's night a traveler* and a Reader of the *If on a winter's night a traveler* that is in *If on a winter's night a traveler.* He is the Reader who is reading *and* read.

Beyond the text, however, there is a Reader who does not have to be read in order to be. Like the Reader who must be read, this Reader also reads *If on a winter's night a traveler, Outside the town of Malbork, Leaning from the steep slope,* and the other fragmentary subfictions, but this Reader also holds an actual copy of *If on a winter's night a traveler* and reads the story of the Reader's readings. Like the Reader who must be read, the Reader who only reads comes to know Ludmilla, Lotaria, Marana, and the other characters in the novel and in the subnovels. But the Reader who must be read can exist only as read; he is equal to and exhausted by the words that describe him. The Reader who need not be read, on the other hand, exists beyond language. This Reader cannot be defined or exhausted by words.

And yet is this true? Is there a Reader beyond language? Both Readers are readers only insofar as they read, and thus both are entangled in words, dependent on language in an essential way. They read, therefore they are. Both Readers exist (as readers) only from the first page of *If on a winter's night a traveler* to the last, and the act which gives them their identity erases them as it consumes the work.

The Reader of/in *If on a winter's night a traveler* is double and yet these Readers are also equal. The "you" of the text is sometimes the Reader who is reading, sometimes the Reader who is read, sometimes both. The distinction between the Reader who is a fiction and the Reader who is a fact is tenuous, for both Readers need the text in order to be who they are. Both read themselves into being.

4

"Yes, a novel that begins like that . . ." he says, "I could swear I've read it. . . ."

In this postmodern age of self-reflexive writing that calls the writer and the act of writing into question, Calvino has expanded the question to include the Reader as well. The who of the Reader becomes as problematic as the who of the writer.

Calvino has asked these questions before, in a number of challenging and convoluted fictions that are as entertaining as they are complex. He is a master storyteller, but he understands that this role is problematic. The best tellers do not expose their tales as fictions; they tell stories as if they were facts, not simply words. But Calvino knows that his stories *are* words and only words, that he alone is responsible for the telling, even when he tells a story that has been told many times before. Thus, he must be present in his tales and absent as well. He must write stories which betray his presence and erase it at the same time.

For this reason, most of his tales are told not by Calvino (as the omniscient narrator) but by fictive storytellers who stand between Calvino and the tales. *The Baron in the Trees*, an early work and one of Calvino's most popular books, is "written" by Biagio, the Baron's brother. The tales in *Cosmicomics* and some of those in *t zero* are told by Qfwfq, an ageless narrator whose stories are memories of his life in the time before time began. The stories in *The Castle of*

Crossed Destinies are told by a deck of Tarot cards and interpreted by any number of tellers, from Lady Macbeth to Hamlet to Faust, and in *Invisible Cities* Marco Polo tells Kublai Khan about ancient cities that may or may not exist beyond the words that describe them. In each of these works, the teller tells tales in which he or she plays a part, and so the act of telling is the proof that the tale is more than just words. The teller tells and is told; he/she speaks him/herself into existence. In addition, the fictional teller helps to hide the fact that both the teller and the act of telling are also told by another, by the author of *The Baron in the Trees, Cosmicomics, t zero, The Castle of Crossed Destinies*: by Italo Calvino.

Who is the teller/writer here? The question becomes more complicated in the novella *The Nonexistent Knight*. This story is written by Sister Theodora, a nun who was once Bradamante, a knight in Charlemagne's army and a major character in the tale she tells. In fact, Sister Theodora tells two stories at once: the story of Algiluf, Raimbaut, Torrismund, Bradamante, and the other warriors in the Christian army and the story of her own struggles in writing the tale. She understands that her role as storyteller is problematic, that "the art of writing tales consists in an ability to draw the rest of life from the nothing one has understood of it, but life begins again at the end of the page when one realizes that one knew nothing whatsoever."[2] Theodora's role is tenuous. She admits that most of her tale is imaginary, and thus she exposes herself *as the teller.* But, as Bradamante, she also tells herself *as the told.* She is both within the tale and without. As Sister Theodora, she is the producer of the story which, in turn, produces her.

2.   Italo Calvino, *The Nonexistent Knight and The Cloven Viscount,* trans. Archibald Colguhoun (New York: Harcourt Brace Jovanovich, 1977), 61.

In fact, the story (an admitted fiction) is the story of Theodora's (real) life. In the tale she writes, Bradamante's lover, Raimbaut, is searching for her, and in the end he finds her in a convent as Sister Theodora, the nun who is writing the story of his search. "That is why my pen at a certain point began running on so. I rush to meet him" (140). Fiction and fact, words and reality collapse into each other.

Who is the writer here? In fact, it is Italo Calvino, carefully hidden behind the story but still present and as problematic as Theodora/Bradamante. And who is the Reader here? The answer seems obvious. The reader is the one whose act of reading makes the story happen. But Theodora is also a reader, for though one might expect that she could tell the tale of Bradamante from memory, still she explains that her story is based on "old unearthed papers or talk heard in our parlor, or a few rare accounts by people who were actually present" (34). She is not actually writing the tale; she is rewriting tales already written and rewritten by others. She can be the writer/teller only because she is first the reader/listener.

All of Calvino's fictional writers are primarily readers rewriting the tales they have read. Biagio's story of his brother's life in the trees is based not on firsthand experience but on tales told to him by others, including the Baron himself. Marco Polo reads the texts of the cities he visits and rewrites (or translates) these texts into words for the Khan. The tellers of *The Castle of Crossed Destinies* read their own stories in the text of the Tarot and tell again what the cards have already told. For each of these tellers, to tell is to tell again what has been told, to write what has been written, to rewrite what has been read.

And like Theodora, Biagio, Polo, and the others, Calvino is also the rewriter of tales that have already been written, tales that he has read. His work has its roots in other texts, in literary genres like science fiction (*Cosmicomics* and *t zero*) and the historical romance (*The Cloven Viscount, The Baron in the Trees, The Nonexistent Knight*). Even his first novel, *The Path to the Nest of Spiders*, published in 1947, is an exercise in and a parody of the boy's adventure genre, as critic Donald Heiney has pointed out.[3] Calvino himself has admitted that this early neorealist work about a child's adventures with the Italian partisan forces during the German Occupation has its roots in *Treasure Island*.[4] *The Path to the Nest of Spiders* is a rewriting of this classic novel, though it is a *Treasure Island* that is aware of itself in a way that Stevenson's original is not. This formal self-consciousness is present in many later Calvino works which have their roots in traditional literary genres but which transcend those genres by self-consciously reproducing them, and the emphasis here is on *re*production. Paradoxically, Calvino's originality lies in his ability to reorder the traditional elements of genre fiction to suit his own purposes; while other novelists feel that they are being creative in their writings, Calvino knows that he is being re-creative, that he is consciously offering variations of stories that have been told before. Some of his parodies, like *The Nonexistent Knight* and *Cosmicomics,* are humorous; others, like *The Path to the Nest of Spiders,* are not. But in each case the work is a reproduction of and within an existing genre which not only reproduces the traditional content but shows how that content fits into its traditional form. The Calvino work is a work of literature laid bare, made transparent, like a perfectly constructed sonnet which explains how a sonnet is to be written.

Genre writers, even self-conscious genre writers who recognize the problematic role they play, are primarily readers,

3. Donald Heiney, "Calvinismo," *Iowa Review* 2 (1971): 80-88.
4. Italo Calvino, *The Path to the Nest of Spiders,* trans. Archibald Colquhoun (New York: Ecco, 1976), xvii.

for it is only by reading that they come to know the rules that make the genre what it is. Calvino is such a reader/writer, as he demonstrates in his *Italian Folktales*, a collection of traditional stories that have been told for centuries and that are told again by Calvino. He can be the writer/teller of these tales only because he has read/heard them many times before, and in fact the folktale is the clearest example of how reading and rewriting come together in the literary work.

In his essay "Myth in the Narrative," Calvino analyzes the meaning of the folktale in terms which also comment on literature in the broader sense. In fact, in its own way this essay is the clearest expression of what Calvino has tried to achieve in his career as a writer. The collection *Italian Folktales* clearly shows that folktales make use of certain basic elements which are repeated again and again: the son or daughter of a peasant, the king, the prince or princess, the quest, the magic weapon, the good fairy, the witch, the evil spell, etc. The number of elements is always strictly limited, and though the structural units themselves may vary from culture to culture, every storyteller must work within the limitations imposed by society. He or she continues to tell stories which are always rooted in tradition and yet always new by combining and recombining these same traditional elements in new ways, much as a composer in the European musical tradition creates new melodies by combining and recombining the same twelve tones of the tempered scale. In a sense, one could say that composers' melodies are not their own; the melodies are already implicit in the scale itself, and composers realize them by exploring the possibilities of what they have been given by their culture.

Calvino makes this same argument with regard to the storyteller. "The narrator explored the possibilities implicit in his own language by combinations and permutations of the characters and actions and the objects on which the characters could accomplish the actions."[5] The folktale, any folktale, is already present in the language the storyteller speaks; he or she does not so much create it as discover it by playing with the basic elements of that language.

For Calvino, the contemporary writer and the primitive storyteller are not so very far apart. What we call literature is only an elaborate and sophisticated folklore, and like the folktale, the literary work is always already present in the author's language. "I believe that all of literature is implicit in language and that literature itself is merely the permutation of a finite set of elements and functions" (76). These functions and elements, of course, are known only to the reader/listener. To write/tell is possible only because the writer/teller has read/listened. The writer is always a reader.

And yet the reader, every reader, is also a writer, for the reader rewrites the text he or she reads in the act of reading. Writers do not create their tales; rather, they re-create them *again*. And readers in their own way also re-create stories. It is in this sense that writing and reading are always forms of recreation.

5

Reading and experience of life are not two universes, but one.

For the Reader in *If on a winter's night a traveler* (the you, the character, the fiction), reading and the desire to read determine his experiences, and yet like his readings, those ex-

5. Italo Calvino, "Myth in the Narrative," trans. Erica Freiberg, in Raymond Federman, ed., *Surfiction: Fiction Now and Tomorrow* (Chicago: Swallow Press, 1975), 75.

periences are only words, not facts but fictions. But for the Reader of *If on a winter's night a traveler* (the real person, you), reading is one experience among others. This Reader is also a worker, lover, sleeper, eater, golfer, swimmer, traveler, watcher, listener, etc., not in a textual world but in a world which seemingly does not need words in order to be.

And yet, just as writers (even writers who base their writings on "real" experiences) are always already immersed in the works of other writers who offer them their language, define their forms, and provide the elements which make writing recognizable *as* writing in a given culture, so readers' nonreading experiences are defined and interpreted by the texts they have read, texts which offer them the language, define the forms, and provide the elements which make life orderly, communicable, and memorable. Readers understand what they read because they have lived, and they understand their lives because they have read.

The worlds of the Reader who reads and the Reader who is read collapse into each other, and in and through *If on a winter's night a traveler* each Reader recognizes himself or herself as reader and as read.

6

. . . there is no certitude outside of falsification.

There is a contradiction at the core of *If on a winter's night a traveler.* On the one hand, the tale is only a tale, only fiction, only words. On the other hand, however, the work goes beyond itself, beyond its printed text and into the text of the Reader's (real) world. This novel is purposely literary, and yet it wants to push against the limits of the literary and break through to a place beyond language.

In fact, as Calvino points out in "Myth in the Narrative," this is not so much a contradiction as the dialectical tension that is the metaphysical ground for the act of writing/reading. The literary work is only words, and yet "the whole struggle of literature is in fact an effort to escape from the confines of language" (77).

The argument is contradictory but true. The narrative urge is and has always been the attempt to speak the unspeakable, to say in a literary context that which is not and cannot be said in everyday language. Calvino states the case perfectly.

Literature is a combinatorial game which plays on the possibilities intrinsic to its own material, independently of the personality of the author. But it is also a game which at a certain stage is invested with an unexpected meaning, a meaning having no reference at the linguistic level on which the activity takes place, but which springs from another level and brings into play something on that other level that means a great deal to the author or to the society of which he is a member. (79)

The "unexpected meaning" is a sacred meaning, for only a sacred text can be more than a text. And the sacred text is a myth, the deepest and most profound expression of a people's view of itself and of its world. Calvino is suggesting not that folklore is popularized or secular myth or that myth and folklore coexist and serve different functions in a culture, but that folklore *preexists* myth and *gives birth to it*, that the sacred is only possible thanks to the secular. According to Calvino's argument, myth is not the basis of a culture but a tear in the cultural fabric, a revolutionary act which does not underlie tradition but destroys it.

And yet this is so only at the moment in which myth arises from the various combinations of folklore; in time, the myth becomes entrenched in the society — it becomes *the* tradition, *the* culture. As such, it soon leaves the original storyteller far behind. "The myth which has sprung from the storyteller's combinatorial game then tends to crystallize, to become a series of set formulas. It passes from the myth-creation stage to a ritualistic phase, from the hands of the storyteller to those of the tribal organization in charge of the preservation and celebration of myths" (80).

The sacred myth, once it is established as such, defines the culture completely and limits every aspect of the society, including the very language which first made the myth possible. The myth closes off many of the old possibilities for the storyteller and forces him to create new ones.

The tribe's sign-system is established in relation to the myth; some signs become taboo and the lay storyteller is no longer allowed to use them directly. He continues to circle around them, inventing new arrangements, until this methodic and objective labor touches off a new illumination of the unconscious and the interdiction, obliging the tribe to find a different system of signs. (80)

By circling the sacred signs, by approaching the point of transgression, the storyteller again attempts to make language say what cannot be said. The teller tries to speak the unspeakable, and, again, these verbal acts border on the revolutionary.

For Calvino's storyteller, narrative is a verbal game but a deeply serious one, for it can disrupt and revolutionize the entire culture. Literature at its best works within the established language and against it at the same time; every such literary work is implicit in the language of the culture, and yet it is also a linguistic impossibility, for it says only what the sign system can say while trying to say more, to push against the limits of mere words. When the combination of elements is right, when the pushing becomes an act of transgression, everything is changed utterly.

If Calvino is right, writers are not engaged in acts of self-expression; rather, they express the possibilities of language at its limits, and their narrative acts say little or nothing about who they are or what they have done with their personal lives. They are not so much creative as re-creative, for they combine and recombine linguistic elements which are not of their own invention. Writing is thus a form of recreation, a game, an entertainment, though at its best it is always something more, something revolutionary. In addition, writing is always on the brink of canceling itself, of erasing what has been written in and through the very act of writing, for, if the narrative succeeds in speaking beyond itself and becoming myth, it destroys the sign system which made it possible. Writing is, in short, a dangerous and self-contradictory activity which must always start over again just as it appears to have reached its goal.

Calvino does not mention the reader in this essay, but, as fellow rewriters and sources of fictions, both the reader and the writer would seem to be involved in a textual realm that is equal to itself and yet transcends itself at the same time. *If on a winter's night a traveler* makes this clear by collapsing the traditional distinctions between writer and reader, the written and the read, fiction and fact, and the novel accomplishes these disruptions by never being what it is and always being what it is not.

If on a winter's night a traveler is the embodiment of the dialectical tension in the act of writing/reading. It is a novel about the unsuccessful search for the novel which documents that search, and as such it is a novel which transcends its own language by erasing itself as it goes along. *If on a winter's night a traveler* is a blatant fiction, so blatant in fact that it becomes real. It would seem that the real *If on a winter's night a traveler* is the physical book the Reader who reads holds and reads. But is it? What if this book is actually another work by another writer, bound by accident in the wrong covers and wrapped in the wrong dust jacket? If the text of *If on a winter's night a traveler* is correct, then it is not the text of *If on a winter's night a traveler*. And if this is not the text of *If on a winter's night a traveler*, then it is a text which is not itself but which exposes itself *as* not itself, and therefore, is itself, just as a liar who admits that he lies is telling the truth.

But does *If on a winter's night a traveler* succeed in breaking free to a place beyond language? In fact, there is no such place, no mythical land beyond time, space, and words. If Calvino's novel transcends its own language, it does so by transforming literary language into something else, by collapsing the language of fiction and the language(s) of fact. *If on a winter's night a traveler* is successful to the extent that it is a repetition which is also different from that which it repeats; it is a self-consciously literary work which expands into the sign systems of the world beyond literature while simultaneously drawing that world, its languages, and their representative (the Reader) into itself.

If on a winter's night a traveler raises many more questions than it answers, and in the act of reading, the Reader poses these questions again. It is in this sense that the novel is successful, though in fact it does not quite succeed in telling a story or in becoming itself. From the opening sentence, *If on a winter's night a traveler* opens a hole in the fabric of the very culture which makes the novel possible.

7

The closing passage of the novel seems to seal that hole.

Now you are man and wife, Reader and Reader. A great double bed receives your parallel reading.

Ludmilla closes her book, turns off her lights, puts her head back against the pillow, and says, "Turn off your light, too. Aren't you tired of reading?"

And you say, "Just a moment, I've almost finished *If on a winter's night a traveler* by Italo Calvino." (260)

If on a winter's night a traveler is at an end. Somehow, the Reader *in* the novel has found the book he wanted to read; in fact, he has created that book from his own adventures, and now he has read it. He has also found a life beyond the novel, in his marriage to Ludmilla, though of course this marriage is as fictive as the fictive Reader's readings. In fact, this Reader vanishes once the book he has written/read is done. He has read himself out of existence.

You, the Reader *of* the novel, also close your copy of the book, and like your fictional counterpart, you too cease to exist (as the Reader), because you have consumed the work that you created and that created you (as the Reader) in turn.

And what remains? You remain, as a Reader in the past but also in the future, as a self-created fiction but also as a fact. And the hole in the fabric of language and culture remains; through it, fiction and fact meet and blend, for the pages you have read are still with you in your life beyond the text, and life and text continue to comment on each other, to question each other, to interact. Your life goes on beyond the novel, but living returns you to these pages (or to others) which again return you to your life. As Sister Theodora/Bradamante/Calvino write(s) in *The Nonexistent Knight*: "A page is good only when we turn it and find life urging along, confusing every page in the book" (140). By this definition, the pages of *If on a winter's night a traveler* are very good indeed.

6

The Author and the I
in the Fiction of J. L. Marcus

this sequence from text is without memory no sex no physical form
written I might be anyone and all of a piece characters in novels
of a nameless first person in author's memories of I's future like the
cycle without landmarks draws its exception of the I it is a structure of memory one critic has argued (in language) by himself one
and the same chronological time and the I has shown freely through
the cycle self person and there is memory and three levels of repetition and the spoken the speaking for all that there realms the level
of the set and the other novels the level of the speaking is in general
in words postmodern consciousness beyond speaking is the producer
and text that is to say while the author speaks the I is not written
but comes into his/her own memories this I himself is the teller/told
he is never spoken he grants omniscient readings or lectures and
his name by the naming the novel itself does not allow for a concept that will be the fiction of the next ten years unavoidable I have
written as they are memories of the past constitute the reader to
understand that present and project into itself as the signifier of
a person at some time form the content produce those texts in

representation of the past person is necessary association outside of the question who is he of the text moves back and forth makes little or no sense as in there is no repetition of memory difference the novels are open to difference and yet demand it fiction has made significant differences interpretation transforms the modernist effort which invites such interpretation definitive examples of a new grid of intersecting and formal innovations of meaning which arise from the self-reflective texts of the cycle not the narrator or those same interpretive answers to the other questions to the question context I is the narrated demonstrated conclusively that author who is separated not a speaking subject and yet itself the I who remembers remaining open

IN THIS OPENING SEQUENCE from his first novel, *Memories of the I's Future,* J. L. Marcus introduces the theme of memory, a concept that will be the focus of five works written over the next ten years.[1] These novels are all of a piece, centered as they are on the life of a nameless first person whose memories of the past constitute both his/her experiences in the present and projections into the future. Like Proust's *A la recherche du temps perdu,* the Marcus cycle draws its content and its form from the content and structure of memory; the representation of the past (in language) is informed by association, outside of chronological time, and the I of the text moves back and forth freely through the already-accomplished. In Marcus, as in Proust, there is memory and repetition of memory, difference within repetition and the repetition of difference.[2] And yet, for all the similarities between *A la recherche du temps perdu* and the Marcus cycle,

1. J. L. Marcus, *Memories of the I's Future* (New York: Grove, 1982); *Exception of the I* (New York: Grove, 1983); *Speaks the I* (New York: Harper and Row, 1985); *Question Context I* (New York: Harper and Row, 1988); *I Who Remembers* (New York: Random House, 1991).
2. For an analysis of repetition and difference in Proust, see Mark D. Seem, "Liberation of Difference: Toward a Theory of Antiliterature," *New Literary History* 5 (1973): 121-34.

there are significant differences which set *Exception of the I, Speaks the I,* and the other novels apart from the modernist effort in general. Marcus' works are definitive examples of a new postmodern consciousness beyond the formal innovations of Joyce, Stein, and Proust and the self-reflective texts of the latter half of the twentieth century.

Unlike Proust's Marcel, the I of the Marcus cycle is not the narrator of his/her own memories. This I is not even the ambiguous teller/told of Raymond Federman's brilliant novels of the seventies and eighties.[3] Rather, in the Marcus context, "I" is the narrated, told by an omniscient, undisclosed author who "is separated from his name by the naming itself."[4] The I who both remembers and is remembered in the same text is without distinguishing features; he/she has no name, no sex, no physical description or age, no occupation or home. I might be anyone. And the same is true for the other characters in Marcus' novels, the various hes, shes, and theys who appear, disappear, and return within the scope of the author's memories of the I's remembering. The text-scape of the cycle is without landmarks, without proper nouns; with the exception of the I, it is a lowercase world.

Although at least one critic has argued that the I, the author, and Marcus himself are one and the same,[5] this clearly

3. Raymond Federman, *Double or Nothing* (Chicago: Swallow Press, 1971); *Take It or Leave It* (New York: Fiction Collective, 1976); *The Voice in the Closet* (Madison: Coda Press, 1979); *The Twofold Vibration* (Bloomington: Indiana University Press, 1982); *Smiles on Washington Square* (New York: Thunder's Mouth Press, 1986); *Enough Is Not Enough* (New York: Harcourt Brace Jovanovich, 1990).

4. Edmond Jabès, "Answer to a Letter," trans. Rosemarie Waldrop, in Don Wellman, ed., *Coherence* (Cambridge, Mass.: O.ARS, 1981), 143–47.

5. C. W. Harrington, "Self/Author/I: The Fiction of J. L. Marcus, *boundary 2* 32 (Spring 1989): 34–50.

is not the case, as Larry McCaffery has shown in his analysis
of the third novel in the cycle, "Self, Person, and Memory in
J. L. Marcus' *Speaks the I*."[6] McCaffery locates three levels
of discourse in the text which he terms the Spoken, the Speaking, and the Unspeakable, and he demonstrates conclusively
that there is no overlap of discursive realms. The level of the
Spoken is, of course, the I, and the level of the Speaking is
the author of the work. The I is, in Roland Barthes' words,
"a paper I,"[7] while the author (the Speaking) is the producer
(though not the product) of the text. That is to say, the I is
spoken without speaking, while the author speaks without ever
being spoken. He is not written but comes into being only
insofar as he is read. Marcus himself is the Unspeakable, and,
though McCaffery does not make this point, the Unspeaking
as well. J. L. Marcus is never spoken; he grants no interviews,
gives no public readings or lectures, and includes no
biographical information or photographs on the dust jackets
of his books. Apart from his name, he does not exist, even
in language. That he is also the Unspeaking seems clear; he
has no need for a voice. If Marcus exists at all, he does so
only in theory, as a hypothetical novelist, for the reader con-
fronted with a literary work invariably assumes that a producer, a writer, is a necessary condition for the very existence
of the text. And yet, as Michel Foucault has shown, this
hypothetical Marcus is not required, is perhaps not even possible. "It would seem that the author's name, unlike other proper
names, does not pass from the interior of a discourse to the
real and exterior individual who produced it; instead, the

6. Larry McCaffery, "Self, Person, and Memory in J. L. Marcus', *Speaks
   the I*," *Sub-Stance* 9 (Fall 1988): 87–92.
7. Roland Barthes, "From Work to Text," in Josué V. Harari, ed., *Textual Strategies: Perspectives in Post-Structuralist Criticism* (Ithaca:
   Cornell University Press, 1979), 79.

name seems always to be present, marking off the edges of the text, revealing, or at least characterizing, its mode of being."[8]

Thus, in the Marcus cycle, the I is a paper I, the author a paper author, and J. L Marcus a paper Marcus, a signifier which need not point beyond itself. Jacques Derrida has noted that "there is no writing which does not devise some means of protection, *to protect against itself*";[9] thus, if there is a J. L. Marcus beyond the name on the dust jacket and the title page (even McCaffery never seems to question his existence), then he has devised the ultimate protection by writing himself out of being. "The writer's presence is thus completely effaced, and what is left is only the words themselves."[10]

It is surprising that so many perceptive critics have overlooked the very real possibility that Marcus does not exist, given that there are any number of references to this possibility in the texts themselves. For example, in *Question Context I,* the author (on McCaffery's level of the Speaking) writes: "the author speaks is not written but comes into his/her own..." Or again, in *I Who Remembers*: "to attend the me the works are in words beyond speaking . . ."

The implication here seems clear, and yet perhaps the point has been passed over because critical language itself does not allow for such a conclusion. Phrases like "the fiction of J. L. Marcus" or "as Marcus says" are almost unavoidable; I have written such things myself and will probably continue to do so. And yet it is important for the reader to understand that the word "Marcus" refers only to itself as the signifier of a

8. Michel Foucault, "What Is an Author?" in Harari, ed., *Textual Strategies*, 147.

9. Jacques Derrida, *Writing and Difference,* trans. Alan Bass (Chicago: University of Chicago Press, 1978), 224.

10. Jerome Klinkowitz, "Avant-garde and After," *Sub-Stance* 9 (1980): 128.

body of texts, not necessarily to a person who, at some time in the past, served as the producer of those texts. In fact, the existence of such a person is neither necessary nor very likely.

Thus, the question "Who is J. L. Marcus in relation to these texts?" makes little or no sense, for one must answer either that there is no J. L. Marcus or that there is no answer. Still, the novels are open to the process of critical questioning, and even demand it, as do so many other works of postmodern fiction. David Porush has made an important point in this regard. "Interpretation transforms the postmodernist text — which invites such interpretation — into an over-determined grid of intersecting, competing, and parallel systems of meaning which arise from and mirror the expectations of the reader."[11]

We have seen how the expectations of the reader have created a J. L. Marcus both within and beyond the texts, and those same interpretive expectations can lead to misguided answers to the other questions implicit in the Marcus cycle, specifically to the question "Who is the I?" McCaffery has demonstrated conclusively that this I is not a narrator, not a speaking subject, and yet who he or she might *be* remains open.

In his brilliant article "The American Voice in the Marcus Cycle," Jerome Klinkowitz has pointed out the allusions to and quotes from the fiction of Nathaniel Hawthorne, Raymond Chandler, Samuel R. Delany, Harry Mathews, Ronald Sukenick, and other American writers that are embedded in the texts of *Memories of the I's Future, Exception of the I,* and *Speaks the I*,[12] and this study has contributed greatly to the understanding of Marcus' work. Still, in his analysis of

11. David Porush, "Technology and Postmodernism: Cybernetic Fiction," *Sub-Stance* 9 (1980): 98.
12. Jerome Klinkowitz, "The American Voice in the Marcus Cycle," *Critical Inquiry* 14 (Fall 1988): 247-53.

the I of these novels, Klinkowitz insists on an unwarranted autobiographical reading. For example, he cites the following passage from *Speaks the I*:

in the cycle in a letter he writes allusions quotes a job he had the other america a department store in the texts of this study reading with sunglasses is misguided understanding recognize his own the I of these novels in question misses the autobiographical reading likely the I of the text having quoted refers to a spelling test in terms of a rather sadistic contention apartment circle horizon bicycle through rough expectations conclusions a single mistake could mean that my sister from a bicycle she was she knew that within her the three years difference turned on those words and this fact it was summer I still remember that terrible voice riding her bicycle she put out her arm to this passage the fact of her body coming down complete and perfect she began to cry I ran to her would seem to be crying correctly the misreading good hand

Having quoted this section, Klinkowitz goes on to discuss it in terms of his own experiences in the classroom of a rather sadistic third-grade teacher. "There was a spelling test every Friday," the critic writes, "and for all of us it was the focal point of the week, because a single mistake could mean a failing grade. She [the teacher] would sit behind her desk, reading the list of words in a colorless monotone but with a frightening smile on her face. She knew that, within her realm, the fate of each of us turned on those words, and she also knew that we knew. I still remember those terrible lists, the words being spoken by that terrible voice. Apartment. Circle. Horizon. Bicycle. Through. Rough. Expectations. Conclusions."

Klinkowitz bases his highly personal interpretation of this passage from *Speaks the I* on the fact that the list of words from one of these third-grade spelling tests is included in the text, complete and in perfect order, though this reading would

seem to be totally without justification.[13] It seems highly unlikely that the I of the text is Jerome Klinkowitz or that the list
of words refers to a spelling test from the critic's past, a test
which Klinkowitz could hardly expect to remember after so
many years. The contention that the author in *Speaks the I*
is Mrs. Kenner, the third-grade teacher, seems equally far-
fetched. No doubt Klinkowitz, for whatever reason, is "reading
into" the Marcus cycle.

It is far more likely that the passage in question refers to
the time when my sister, Nicole, broke her arm in a fall from
a bicycle. She was nine years old, and I was twelve (the "three
years difference" in the Marcus text confirms this fact). It was
a summer afternoon, shortly after my father had come home
from work but before supper, and she was riding her bicycle
up the driveway. As she passed my father's parked car, she
lost her balance and fell against the door. She put out her
arm to break her fall, and the weight of her body coming
down at such an angle on one hand caused a fracture near
the elbow.

I saw what happened, and, when she began to cry, I ran
to her, calling to my parents who came running out of the
house. My sister stood up, her face flushed, crying pitifully,
holding the broken arm with her good hand as if she were
trying to keep the fractured bone in place. My mother and
father reached her and began talking so loudly and question-

13. This particular sequence would seem to be especially difficult to in-
terpret correctly. The misreading on the part of so eminent a thinker
as Jerome Klinkowitz surprises me, though he is not the only critic
to have missed the point here. In a recent letter, Larry McCaffery
writes that this same passage is a direct allusion to a job he had as
a student selling sunglasses in a department store in a large midwestern
city. He agrees with me that Klinkowitz's reading is misguided, and
yet he has since refused to recognize that his own interpretation of
the sequence in question misses the mark completely.

ing her with such concern that their voices ran together in a blur of sound. I stood off to one side and watched. There was nothing I could have done to keep my little sister from falling, and so I knew that I could not be blamed for what had happened to her. Perhaps it was for that reason that I could hardly keep from laughing. I wasn't happy, of course. I loved my sister very much, and even now, after so many years, Nicole and I are still very close. It hurt me to see that she was in pain. It hurts me now to remember. And yet, at the time, her tears seemed funny to me. Her red face was like a comical mask, and my parents' excitement and confusion only made the situation seem like a frantic scene from an old slapstick movie.

I couldn't laugh out loud, of course. My sister was hurt, my mother and my father were upset, and I cannot imagine what they would have thought of me if I had let out so much as a chuckle. My parents probably would have thought that somehow my sister's accident had been my fault, that I had pushed her or let air out of her bicycle tires. I had done nothing, of course, but as I stood there, watching my mother and father put my sister into the back seat of the car, I felt guilty, as if I *had* been the cause of everything that had happened. My father got behind the wheel, my mother sat beside him, and they drove off to the hospital emergency room, leaving me alone. Once they were gone, I was free to laugh, but I no longer saw the joke.

It seems clear that the quoted passage from *Speaks the I* refers to this incident and, in fact, recounts it in some detail. Because the Marcus technique often involves the repetition of the same scene from various perspectives, it is not surprising that my sister's accident recurs several times in the cycle, thus confirming my original interpretation. I offer an example from *Question Context I*:

trying refers to this incident and father reacher her and began because the technique with the same scene from various blur of sound I stood off my sister's accident nothing I could have done to thus confirm my original falling and so I knew that I from again the details of had happened to her perhaps in a form which reproduces I could hardly keep from laughing certainly the above I loved my sister very much and not as the story hurts me himself who drives a buick her tears seemed funny to me snow storm there is a relaxed mark and my parents' excitement through the cycle situation of the accident story when I couldn't laugh keep my little sister from interpretation I offer blame for what the story presents reason transforms the original I wasn't happy of course once again even now after so many years perhaps to remember and yet at the time over a cliff during a red fact like comical incident that recurs in fragments and confusion repeating one important scene I took her hand and tried to laugh in her face they were gone I was free I care for her very much and the joke seems clear

Again, the details of the story are present, though in a form which both reproduces and transforms the original telling. Certainly the above refers once again to my sister's accident and not, as Raymond Federman insists in his "Colter/Altier/Marcus: The Threefold Vibration" to the story of someone (perhaps Federman himself) who drives a Buick Special over a cliff during a snowstorm.[14]

There is a related incident that recurs in fragments throughout the cycle, repeating one important theme of the accident story. When I was eighteen, I dated a tall, dark-haired girl whose father died quite unexpectedly a few weeks before Christmas. I was expected to attend the wake, and, as I entered the small, softly lit viewing room, I saw the girl and her family sitting in the front row. I waited for a mo-

14. Raymond Federman, "Colter/Altier/Marcus: The Threefold Vibra-tion," in Welch D. Everman, ed., *Postmodern Fiction and the Crisis of the Self* (London: Routledge and Kegan Paul, 1990), 23-53.

ment at the back, and suddenly, as if she sensed that I was there, the girl turned in her seat and looked at me. I could see that she had been crying, but for some reason, when she saw me standing there, she started to cry again.

I wanted to laugh. I could hardly control myself, and I knew that if I went to her, if I took her hand and tried to tell her how sorry I was, I would laugh in her face. There was no explanation for it. I cared for her very much, and I had liked her father. Perhaps my desire to laugh was a defense against the oppressive scene, the candles and the flowers, the many solemn people I didn't know, and the familiar face in the open casket. Or perhaps it was only that I knew laughter was the most inappropriate response I could make in the situation, the one thing I could not afford to do.

She was still looking at me, waiting for me, but I turned and left. Out in the parking lot behind the funeral parlor, alone in my car, I laughed until I cried. I never saw the tall, dark-haired girl again.

In the Marcus cycle, there are a number of brief references to this incident. For example, on page 30 of *Memories of I's Future,* the author writes: "the dark-haired girl whose father hurt my mother and my father weeks before christmas I could see that she and father put my sister into reason when she saw me . . ." This same passage is repeated, word for word, on page 217 of *I Who Remembers,* and on page 316 of *Question Context I* one finds the following: "I felt guilty as if I *had* wanted to laugh I had my father knew leaving me alone was no explanation for it to laugh but I no longer saw . . ."

Unfortunately, there is no detailed presentation of the incident anywhere in the five novels, though it seems clear that the cycle is moving in that direction. It will be interesting to see what Marcus has to say in this regard when his novel-in-progress, *His Own the I,* is published.

Index

A la recherche du temps perdu
(Proust), 129
Amer Eldorado (Federman), 36
Anselm, 34-35, 38, 41, 47, 48
Apollinaire, Guillaume, 78
Automatic writing, 28, 32

Baron in the Trees, The
(Calvino), 116, 119
Barthes, Roland, xiii, xiv, xv, xvi,
xvii, 101-2, 104, 131
Bataille, Georges, 78, 101, 103,
106
Beckett, Samuel, 36-39, 80, 103,
107; *Molloy*, 36-38
Benabou, Marcel, 67
Big Sur (Kerouac), 25
Blanchot, Maurice, xv, 101, 106,
107
Book of Dreams (Kerouac), 25
Borges, Jorge Luis, 80, 103
Broch, Hermann, 4

Calvino, Italo, xvii, 67-68, 75-76,
80, 86, 107, 108, 111-27; *Baron
in the Trees, The*, 116, 119;

*Castle of Crossed Destinies,
The*, 107, 116-17, 118; *Cloven
Viscount, The*, 119, *Cosmi-
comics*, 116, 119; *If on a
winter's night a traveler*, xvii,
111-27; *Invisible Cities*, 117;
Italian Folktales, 120; "Myth in
the Narrative," 120-21, 123-24;
Nonexistent Knight, The,
117-18, 119, 127; *Path to the
Nest of Spiders, The*, 119; *t
zero*, 116, 117, 119
Cantor, Jay, 14-25, 26, 30, 32,
33; *Death of Che Guevara,
The*, 14-23
Cassady, Neal, 23-33. *See also*
Moriarty, Dean; Pomeray, Cody
Castle of Crossed Destinies, The
(Calvino), 107, 116-17, 118
Castro, Fidel, 14-15, 22
Céline, Louis-Ferdinand, 3-4
Ceremonies of Love (Peckinpah),
83, 85
Chained to Desire (Herty), 95
Chandler, Raymond, 133
Charters, Ann, 25n

Cloven Viscount, The (Calvino), 119

Complete Bolivian Diaries of Che Guevara and Other Captured Documents (Guevara), 15

Constrictive forms, 67-71; lipogram, 69-70; palindrome, 69; perverb, 74-75; sonnet, 68-69

Coover, Robert, 4; *Public Burning, The,* 4

Cortázar, Julio, 80, 107; *Hopscotch,* 107

Cosmicomics (Calvino), 116, 119

Cosmoeroticism, 98

Death of Che Guevara, The (Cantor), 14-23

de Berg, Jean, 91; *Image, The,* 91

Delany, Samuel R., 133

de Mandiargues, Andre Pierye, 84, 91; *Motorcycle, The,* 91

Derrida, Jacques, 80, 132

Desolation Angels (Kerouac), 25

Dharma Bums (Kerouac), 25

Discursive shift, 6-10

Disparition, La (Perec), 70-71, 76

Docufiction, xvi, 3-33

Double or Nothing (Federman), 36, 38, 40, 42, 46-54, 59

Evil: pornography and, 96-97; Marquis de Sade and, 100-102

Exception of the I (Marcus), 130, 133

Executioner's Song, The (Mailer), 4-14, 16, 23

Fast, Howard, 4

Federman, Raymond, xvi, 34-61, 130, 137; *Amer Eldorado,* 36; *Double or Nothing,* 36, 38, 40, 42, 46-54, 59; *Journey to Chaos,* 36; *Smiles on*

Washington Square, 36, 42; *Take It or Leave It,* 36, 40, 42, 50-54, 59; *Twofold Vibration, The,* 36, 40, 42, 55-56, 58, 59; *Voice in the Closet, The,* 36, 55, 56-58, 59

Finnegans Wake (Joyce), 107

Folktale, 120-24

Foster, Hal, xvi

Foucault, Michel, 18-19, 20, 22, 66, 80, 88, 131-32

Getting Into Each Other (Stearns), 78, 85

Gilmore, Gary, 4-15, 17, 22-23, 25, 27, 33

Grand Rhetoriqueurs, 68

Guerilla Warfare (Guevara), 15

Guevara, Ernesto (Che), 14-23, 25, 27, 30, 33; *Complete Bolivian Diaries of Che Guevara and Other Captured Documents,* 15; *Guerilla Warfare,* 15; *Reminiscences of the Cuban Revolutionary War,* 15; *Venceremos!* 15

Hawthorne, Nathaniel, 133

Heine, Maurice, 105

Heiney, Donald, 119

Herty, Andrea, 95

His Own the I (Marcus), 138

Hopscotch (Cortázar), 107

If on a winter's night a traveler (Calvino), xvii, 111-27

Image, The (de Berg), 91

Infinite text, 13; pornography as, 80-81, 86, 88-89, 99-101, 103, 105-8

Invisible Cities (Calvino), 117

Italian Folktales (Calvino), 120

I Who Remembers (Marcus), 132, 138